CHOICES
of the
HEART

Christian Ethics for Today

DOUGLAS D. WEBSTER

*Zondervan*Publishing*House*
Academic and Professional Books
Grand Rapids, Michigan

*A Division of HarperCollins*Publishers

Choices of the Heart
Copyright © 1990 by Douglas D. Webster

ACADEMIE BOOKS is an imprint of Zondervan Publishing House,
1415 Lake Drive, S.E., Grand Rapids, Michigan 49506

Library of Congress Cataloging in Publication Data

Webster, Douglas D.
    Choices of the heart / Douglas Webster.
      p.   cm.
    Includes index.
    ISBN 0-310-34801-3
    1. Christian ethics. 2. Christian life–1960- 3. United States-
-Moral conditions.   I.Title.
    BJ1251.W33   1990
    241–dc20   90-36844
                               CIP

All Scripture quotations, unless otherwise indicated, are taken from the
Holy Bible: New International Version (North American Edition).
Copyright © 1973, 1978, 1984 by the International Bible Society. Used
by permission of Zondervan Bible Publishers.

Edited by Susan E. McShane and Leonard G. Goss
Designed by Jan M. Ortiz

Printed in the United States of America

90 91 92 93 94 95 / PP / 10 9 8 7 6 5 4 3 2 1

*To Jeremy, Andrew, Kennerly,
may you act justly, love mercy,
and walk humbly with your God.*

CONTENTS

INTRODUCTION

Choices of the Heart is a challenge. It will move you beyond the religiously and culturally conditioned habits of the heart and encourage you to cultivate the wisdom and discernment needed to live as you ought to live.

All too often we begin ethics by discussing the controversial "issues" without addressing the ethic behind our ethics. In the process of taking sides on abortion, capital punishment, nuclear weapons, homosexual partnerships, euthanasia, and any number of other hot topics, we avoid the fundamental question of Christian character.

There are many moral issues that should concern us deeply. Before we can deal meaningfully with these issues, we need to begin the process of internalizing the wisdom revealed by God. We need to gain a perspective that sees the larger moral picture from the horizon of God's will. As a father and a pastor I am concerned that we begin ethical reflection, not with a list of issues, but with Christian character.

My children are pretty impressionable. They look at children a few years older than they are and try to copy their dress and manner. Everyone wants to be cool. The other day Kennerly, our four-year-old daughter, got into the car after spending the afternoon at a friend's house. Her socks were neatly rolled down below her ankles and her hair was fixed just like the teenage girl who had been watching her. "You look different," I said. "I like your socks and hair." Kennerly tossed her head confidently and said, "That's cool! Dad. I look just like Sara!" "Why do you want to be like Sara?" I asked. "Do you think Sara is good on the inside?" Kennerly swished her hair, wrinkled up her nose, and said, "Who cares about that? Nobody sees it." Kennerly underscored the fact that we tend to live by appearances; how we look is more important than who we are. It is easier, after all, to copy somebody's image than to build character. Today's prevailing philosophy is simple enough for a four-year-old to grasp. The world wants her to live by appearances. I want to help her live by her convictions. And not just any convictions will do. These convictions must be shaped by the wisdom of God if they are to be life-fulfilling. My wife Ginny and I want all three of our children to grow beyond being cool to being wise. The chances of this happening are slim if they do not see in their parents the quality of life and character intended by God, modeled in Christ, and empowered by the Holy Spirit.

I am a pastor in Bloomington, Indiana. Our church is a few blocks from Indiana University and its thirty-three thousand students. Hundreds of students attend our church every Sunday. They study and play in a moral environment that is diametrically opposed to a Christian ethic. SAT scores may measure intelligence but there is no easy test designed to measure moral maturity. Many of our students have never been taught to think Christianly about sex and intimacy, leisure and sports, success and money. Their Christian faith is compartmentalized in a cubicle reserved for religious feelings and private sentiment. They may have an emotional Christianity but they do not have an ethical Christianity. They may know how to look cool in "secular circles" and "Christian circles" but they lack the depth to "take captive every thought to make it obedient to Christ" (2 Cor. 10:5). The reason many students are this way is that their parents are this way. Parents have abdicated their moral responsibility and become spiritual couch potatoes feasting on a diet of pop Christianity. Is it any wonder that students get blown away spiritually and morally when they hit campus?

I hope *Choices of the Heart* will make you more aware of your own character. It is designed to provoke your thinking and challenge how you do ethics. "The ethic behind the ethics" may strike you as a curious phrase, but it captures something important. If we do not think first of the shape of Christian character, how can we handle all the data of ethical issues? Moral maturity is not a matter of more information and better strategies of indoctrination. The bottom line is character. The educated heart shares God's deep aspirations for justice and righteousness and applies these convictions to ordinary life. Life is placed in orbit around a quality of being that reflects spiritual devotion, ethical discernment, and a teachable spirit. Character is not assembled, it is nurtured. Christians with an educated heart do not fall off an assembly line. They are grown in the soil of spiritual transformation and the whole counsel of God.

True character is reflected in the lives of those who have learned the moral will of God by heart. They work out the will of God the way a gifted musician plays music. I have a good friend who is completing his doctorate in piano at Indiana University. What is special about Paul is not only that he can play a complex musical score with masterly precision but also that he feels and knows the music. He plays for our worship on Sunday morning with a heart for music that goes well beyond the mechanics of playing a piece. The way Paul makes music is the way I want to live ethically.

Without a unified field theory of moral reflection and action we are pulled and jerked from one issue to another. We feel guilty when besieged by the activist whose single issue has become the dominant concern of his life. We are tempted to join him in his holy war and devote all of our resources and energy to the crusade. But moral-order living and Christian spirituality prevent us from reducing moral passion to a single ethical issue. It is deceptively easy to mount a moral campaign to clean up our country but in the process blatantly violate Jesus' kingdom ethic. The primary moral thrust of the Christian community belongs not to those who can shout the loudest and organize the biggest demonstration but to those who reveal the character of the Lord Jesus Christ in every area of life.

Many today feel confused by the unraveling complexity of contemporary ethical issues. We seem buried under an avalanche of information, rhetoric, and opposing opinions. Instead of making wise choices we settle for moral decorum. We remain confused and apathetic. This book does not promise to undo all the complexity of today's ethical issues, but it seeks to redirect our focus. We will explore the roots of wisdom and the qualities of a discerning heart that enable a person to be wise and to make courageous choices. Through ancient case studies we will see the practical meaning of moral-order character. We will consider David's moral legacy and Absalom's strategy of success. We will reflect on Solomon's simple request for wisdom and his pathetic moral demise.

Choices of the Heart examines the cultural influences that shape our moral decision making. If we are committed to developing Christian character, we will find ourselves contending with moralistic thinking on the one hand and relativistic thinking on the other. The first obstacle is religious, self-righteous, fearful, and militant. The second barrier is secular, pleasure seeking, confident, and aggressive. Both wage war against the moral character commended in the Word of God and the life of Jesus.

The ethic behind the ethics roots decision making in a life commitment to the fear of God, not man; the lordship of Christ, not self; the whole counsel of God, not the opinions of man; and the ethic of the Cross, not the expediency of the moment. Christian commitment radicalizes the choices of the heart. Contrary to popular opinion and religious legalism, the Word of God does not remove the freedom of choice; it strengthens it. Those who advocate the freedom to do whatever they want devalue decision making. The freedom to choose anything at any time renders choice meaningless because it strips from decision making any sense of commitment. For example, the meaningful choice of a vowed life-commitment in marriage is shattered when one reserves the right to choose additional sexual partners in search of intimacy. True freedom is as liberating as it is limiting. It is the freedom to choose righteousness and holiness. It is not the freedom to do just anything. This book argues against the devaluation of choice and the deresponsibilizing of the human person.

Our moral decisions matter because they matter to God and determine the direction of our lives. What we decide is not arbitrary and inconsequential. The choices of the heart are choices between life and death. They reveal our character. Those who guard their hearts with the life morality of God's commands really know life (Prov. 4:23) and those who set apart Christ as Lord in their hearts experience salvation (1 Peter 3:15). The ancient challenge God set before Israel remains before all those who follow the Lord Jesus Christ:

> See, I set before you today life and prosperity, death and destruction. For I command you today to love the LORD your God, to walk in his ways, and to keep his commands, decrees and laws; then you will live. . . . But if your heart turns away and you are not obedient, and if you are drawn away to bow down to other gods and worship them, I declare to you this day that you will certainly be destroyed. . . . This day I call heaven and earth as witnesses against you that I have set before you life and death, blessings and curses. Now choose life, so that you and your children may live and that you may love the LORD your God, listen to his voice, and hold fast to him. For the LORD is your life. . . . (Deut. 30:15–20)

The questions at the end of each chapter are designed to deepen your reflection, provoke your thinking, and help you shape your perspective. You may wish to gather some friends together and work through the questions.

Choices of the Heart is an offering of spiritual direction that grows out of a community of believers who have character. Thanks to Mark and Linda Wisen for a place in the sun to finish the manuscript. Tim Bayless provided not only a computer but thoughtful perspective. My friend and colleague Jim Eschenbrenner offered helpful insight. Jim Meals, Terry Black, Bill van Antwerpen, John Long, and Louise Webster all made valuable suggestions for improving the manuscript. As always, Ginny remains my best counsel and encouragement.

1

Choices of the Heart

If life is so easy, why do we find living so difficult? We
imagine life becoming more fulfilling and meaningful as
time goes on. Once we work through our adolescent
confusion and our career options, we say to ourselves, then
we will be able to settle down and enjoy life. After we have
established our relational bearings then we hope we will
know how to shape the other aspects of our lives. The sad
truth, however, is that millions of us who are married and
not divorced, adequately paid and moderately satisfied with
our jobs, still find life depressingly difficult and unreward-
ing. We live in such a material world that our happiness
and satisfaction seem almost unnaturally tied to "things"

and "events." Our relational world is not much better. It is only a matter of time before the life we have painstakingly put together falls apart. There is no safety net for heartbreak. We have insurance for everything but peace and joy.

What is it that makes living more difficult in a culture striving to make life more comfortable? How can we explain, let alone affect, divorce and suicide rates, the plague of substance abuse, and the pervasive problem of sexual fixation and addiction? Evidently something vital is missing in the American dream.

The Danish Christian philosopher Søren Kierkegaard, commenting on European culture in the 1840s, observed, "Everything goes on as usual, and yet there is no longer any one who believes in it." In the 1990s the scene is changing and the thin veneer of normality is wearing through. Kierkegaard saw then what we must see today: "The invisible spiritual bond which gives it validity no longer exists, and so the whole age is at once comic and tragic—tragic because it is perishing, comic because it goes on."[1]

Comfort and Convenience

North American culture is designed to make life easy. Our aim is comfort and convenience, and we work hard at it. Immediate gratification, pleasurable work, and images of success are on everyone's daily agenda. We live in a "can do" society where anything is possible if we put our mind to it and back it with money. In the words of Paul Simon:

> These are days of lasers in the jungle, staccato signals
> of constant information where medicine is magi-
> cal. . . . These are the days of miracle and wonder."[2]

[1]Søren Kierkegaard, "Either/Or: A Fragment of Life" in *A Kierkegaard Anthology,*ed. Robert Bretall (Princeton, N.J.: Princeton University Press, 1946), pp. 81–82.
[2]Paul Simon, "The Boy in the Bubble," from *Graceland* (Warner Brothers Records, 1986).

Our culture makes it easy for us to communicate faster, travel farther, live longer, play harder, and have more fun. But we are finding it difficult to practice the virtues of living. Knowing and obeying truth, being faithful in marriage, enjoying the rhythm of life, knowing how to parent and how to grow old have become less attainable goals. When we hear the word *fidelity* we think first of our stereo systems, not our marriages. We find ourselves debating whether certain techniques extend life or prolong dying, but little is said about preparing for a "good death" in a spiritual sense.

Through the eyes of many people from other cultures, North America is a paradise. We communicate by cellular phone and satellite. We worry about dieting instead of famine. Interest rates receive more publicity than poverty. What other cultures dream of having we accept as commonplace—drinking water, sewage treatment, electrical power, central air, medical care, and public education. Our upscale middle-class homes are a wealthy landowner's dream in Argentina or India.

A few years ago my family and I moved from Toronto, Canada, to a small town in America's heartland. We left behind the traffic and hassles of urban life, in exchange for the relatively stress-free living of Bloomington, Indiana. Our first impression was that life was so much easier in a town of fifty-six thousand. Instead of a daily routine of getting to work through twenty-one traffic lights and bumper-to-bumper frustration, now I arrived in ten minutes.

Even in one of the most beautiful, crime-free cities in North America, life in Toronto seemed rougher and more demanding. Ginny and I used to debate the safety of our children walking to school. It was not only the traffic we were concerned about; we were afraid some "crazy" might mug our child en route. We appreciated the demands placed on teachers whose classes were largely made up of children from broken homes. Single-parent families, latch-key kids, live-in boyfriends, and easy access to drugs were all part of the urban mosaic. In the summer a steady stream of homosexual men parked their cars on our street, made their way to the end of our street, and descended the cliffs overlooking Lake Ontario to a popular gay beach.

The city also brought with it an economic intensity foreign to Smalltown U.S.A. We moved four times before we bought our first home. We went from a very noisy, cockroach-infested, one-bedroom apartment to a much quieter, cleaner, and better-managed two-bedroom apartment. However we gladly left the high rises for a small town house on the outskirts of the city. Even though we regularly heard our neighbor's yelling or snoring through the thin walls, it was better than an apartment, especially with children. When we bought our small detached home on a lot twenty-five feet wide and one hundred feet long, we were pleased. It was more in the city and close to the church we were involved in. The mortgage seemed astronomical, but it was better than paying close to the same amount in rent with nothing to show for it. The value of that little home doubled in the three years we lived there, requiring the new owners to finance a mortgage nearly triple what ours had been. No wonder property values, interest rates, and rent controls were hot conversational topics in Toronto. We gladly gave up that pressure by moving to the Midwest.

"Toronto, the Good" (the nickname was acquired years ago in more conservative times) is a virtual babel of languages, races, ethnic groups, and moralities. It was exciting and challenging to live there, but we imagined it would be easier to live in Bloomington and bring up our children in a small university town. After we moved we learned that Bloomington was rated seventh in the nation out of 250 cities for low stress and was recognized as one of the best towns in America for retirees. Home to 33,000 students at Indiana University, Bloomington afforded a rare combination of intellectual and artistic stimulation, cultural and sporting events, affordable housing, and a small town atmosphere that wasn't too small-minded. In many respects it is the epitome of easy-living, American life. But I have come to have serious reservations about the quality of life in America's Heartland.

By making life easier for ourselves we do not make life better. We may remove the hassles of traffic, long lines, and crowds of people. We may reduce economic and work pressure and eliminate "adjusting" to ethnic diversity. We may live in a more "user-friendly" atmosphere and enjoy more personable relationships, but that does not necessarily develop our character, deepen our spirituality, and make us more sensitive ethically.

Religion thrives in Bloomington but so does self-righteousness and fear. Churches are well attended but basketball means more. The urban passion for getting ahead is replaced by the suburban passion for having fun. The time freed up from traffic and routine city life is channeled into the pursuit of pleasure to overcome the boredom of daily life. Life is a collage of activities randomly connected to offer the appearance of fulfillment and meaning.

Children are attended to, even fussed over. Their success is important, but "success" is defined in societal terms, not in spiritual qualities. Some parents are doing their job if their children turn out reasonably well-adjusted, happy, religiously sensible, and sports-minded. Being good tends to be defined more by what children don't do. They don't take drugs, they don't sleep with their boyfriend or girlfriend, they don't rebel.

Some parents work frantically to insulate their children from the evil forces of secular humanism so that they will not rebel and embarrass them. They would consider that allowing their children to attend public school would be like offering their children on the altar of the god Molech. They consider the Midwest to be a bastion against East Coast liberalism and West Coast permissiveness, but even here they fear the pagan public school system will corrupt their children morally and cause them to grow up disbelieving that Creation took place in six twenty-four-hour days. For such parents everyone who is not a politically conservative fundamentalist is under suspicion. They want to assure themselves that their children will grow up to think and act as they do. The more they control the relational and educational environment, the easier it is for them to cope with life.

Smalltown U.S.A. seems intent on reducing life to the lowest and broadest common denominator. Life is easier that way, less confusing. Peer group pressure is intensified for all ages. It is a "copycat" culture both in appearance and mentality, the latter being the less noticed but the more dangerous. Christian teaching is essentially innocuous, carefully measured out in small dosages, and anecdotally applied—the more entertaining the better. The "audience," for that is what many congregations have become, is much more concerned with the personality of the speaker than with the depth of the content. The speaker's jokes will be remembered long after the truth of the message.

Felt-needs have a virtual monopoly on preaching. To stray from issues that do not appear immediately relevant to the "me" generation (intent on getting home for the NFL game of the week), is to invite criticism. Constant repetition of religious clichés has become a necessity to reassure the religious consumer that they are shopping at the right place and getting the right product. People can tune in and tune out countless times during the Sunday morning sermon and still get the message because they have heard it so many times before. We have made it a religious virtue to make it easy for the "believer." Our ecclesiastical planning and programing is carried out with a marketing mentality designed to get and keep the numbers. We are spectators, not servants, shopping for the lowest-priced religion in town. Sentiment, not spirituality, reinforces our way of life.

I have come to the conclusion that easy living is not making it any easier to live. We are nice, cordial people. We have the social graces but our homes have become combat zones. As a culture we are broken, addicted, lonely, and lustful, but on camera we are everyone's envy. Who can understand our fascination with fashion, our flippancy with fidelity, our spectator passion for sports, and our boredom with everyday life? Where is the life we have lost in living?

A brief look at three institutions in our culture may serve to illustrate the current triviality of the choices of the heart and the profound need we have for moral character.

On Camera

Next to weapons and computers, movies are one of America's billion dollar exports. We are the entertainment capital of the world, putting our fun-loving, thrill-seeking culture on display in almost every nook and cranny in the global village. A friend of mine who lives in the Ivory Coast tells me that this small African country virtually shuts down to watch "Dallas." In a culture devoted to eradicating pain, we have a seemingly insatiable appetite for television violence and celluloid laughter.

We are "amusing ourselves to death," claims communications theorist Niel Postman. Serious, rational discourse has a hard time getting off the ground. Our media-conditioned culture, Postman argues, has "adjusted to incoherence and been amused into indifference."[3]

The philosophers in the age of entertainment are political pollsters, market consultants, talk show hosts, fashion designers, sports commentators, and advertisers. They have more influence on morality than anyone else and they are heard by more people, but this new version of morality follows trends rather than truths. Opinion polls pull more weight than proven precepts. Cosmetics and humor go further in advancing ideas than character and honor, and flexibility is a greater virtue than fidelity.

"Even though life is quite a sad business," writes novelist Mary Gordon, "you can have a good time in the

[3]Niel Postman, *Amusing Ourselves to Death: Public Discourse in the Age of Show Business* (New York: Penguin Books, 1985), pp. 110–11.

middle of it."[4] But many in the middle of their "good time" challenge even that optimism. In these days of miracle and wonder, Paul Simon's consoling words "Don't cry baby, don't cry" are simultaneously both out of place and yet quite appropriate. As a culture we are like the rich fool Jesus talked about: he had mastered the art of limited liabilities but lost his soul.

In a culture that sells moral virtue to obtain the tangibles of material success, we are having real trouble seeing the value of the soul and the reality of God. If it cannot be televised, advertised, and computerized, it's not worth having. By common consent we have agreed on a host of distractions from insurance premiums to body-building. Anything that will get our mind off who we are and what are we living for is marketable in a culture that desperately wishes to laugh and forget. Humor and shopping, sports and eating, have become essential distractions for living.

Cultural historian and social analyst Christopher Lasch argues that everyday life in these troubled times becomes an exercise in survival. Just maintaining our emotional equilibrium causes us to withdraw and attempt to escape. The "survival strategies forced on those exposed to extreme adversity" such as war, imprisonment, famine, and plague serve as the pattern for daily survival in a culture with around-the-clock entertainment, religious liberty, supermarkets and shopping malls. Lasch suggests that the techniques for coping with this feeling of vulnerability include "selective apathy, emotional disengagement from others, renunciation of the past and the future, a determination to live one day at a time."[5] If we cannot control the big, impersonal, bureaucratic world that seeks to control us, then at least we can try to control ourselves.

---

[4]Mary Gordon, "Growing up Catholic and Creative," *U.S. News and World Report*, (October 5, 1987).

[5]Christopher Lasch, *The Minimal Self: Psychic Survival in Troubled Times* (New York: Norton, 1984), p. 57.

Consider the irony of our culture: We are insulated from much of the suffering and trauma of war, terrorism, famine, and disease known to the rest of the world—yet we concentrate on survival strategies. We may live outwardly successful lives but inwardly we are empty and lonely. It is as if we had struck a Faustian bargain with the devil. In exchange for peace and prosperity, pleasure and power, we have sold our collective soul to the devil. We have traded the power of truth for the power of technique, the habits of the soul for the habits of self-centeredness, self-mastery for self-rule, and eternal joy for immediate happiness.

External threats such as nuclear war, terrorism, and economic collapse overshadow our peace and prosperity, but the real threat comes from within. Our world is imploding. In a material world guided by convenience and self-satisfying preservation the absence of morality creates a vacuum.

If we are becoming imprisoned in a brave new world of technique and selfish autonomy, it is a world of our own making. It is not just happening to us, we are creating it. Civilization is being driven by the habits of self-centered individualism, the instincts of depravity, and the techniques of self-management. Freedom of individual choice has superceded the pursuit of justice. On camera our moral confusion is painfully obvious. We don't know whether to laugh or cry.

On Campus

Commenting on education at Harvard, Robert Coles said, "We have systems here to explain everything except how to live. And we have categories for every person on earth, but we cannot explain one person."[6] When students decide which university to attend on the reputation that it is a "partying" school or because alumni boast that "sports

[6]Robert Coles, quoted by Philip Yancey, "The Crayon Man," in *Christianity Today* (February 6, 1987), p. 20.

is the glue that holds the university together," something is wrong in our approach to education. Walker Percy said it well: "Students are getting all A's but flunking ordinary life!"[7]

I overheard a group of college students in a restaurant laughing about a performance of *Born Free* that they did back in high school. It was comical to them to recall their youthful exuberance, belting out heroic lyrics about being free and life being worth living. After a few years of college they mocked their innocence and naïveté. I suppose Bruce Springsteen's "Born in the U.S.A." is more appropriate for today; it is a song of despair sung with earthy gusto. My seven-year-old rocks to its strong beat without the foggiest notion that it is about Vietnam, unemployment, and death. We have managed to memorialize a passionate song of despair without any sadness over its moral realism. Even our messages of anguish get turned into star material and commercial success. The American Dream is so all-pervasive and the quest for comfort so vigorous that even our nihilism, our despair of life itself, becomes a proud performance and a badge of identity worn by affluent suburban young people who are morally illiterate.

The missing element in the North American Dream is character. We no longer know who we are or who we should be. There is little basis for moral order either in public life or in our personal lives. When attempts are made to understand common goodness in acts of kindness and virtue offered to us by friends or strangers, we value our theories of conditioning more than our intrinsic moral conscience and spiritual worth. When our biggest questions are "What should we wear?" and "What are we going to do Saturday night?" the vital signs of moral character are missing. We are reduced to the habits of the self-centered personality.

We are driven by data but default on discernment. We

[7]Walker Percy from *The Second Coming*, quoted by Philip Yancey, "The Crayon Man," *Christianity Today*, (Feburary 6, 1987), p. 17.

have so much knowledge but so little wisdom, and the information we seem to need for living minimizes moral courage and conviction. We demand instant global access to knowledge without regard for virtue.

Moral confusion is automatic when value-free instruction becomes the necessary goal in elementary school sex education classes and Ivy League professional schools. True pluralism allows for public discussion and the debate of competing ideas rather than the elimination of meaningful dialogue and moral conviction.

Ethics tends to be reduced to compliance with the law or professional etiquette. Consequently, no matter how many ethics courses are added to business school curricula, we will still be unable to discern between good and evil, justice and injustice. James Laney, President of Emory University, observes:

> We seem to be turning out people who are bent on exploiting careers for their own ends rather than service through their professions for the sake of society. And that is exactly what we are bound to do if we do not educate the heart, without virtue, without education of the heart, expertise and ambition easily become demonic.[8]

In *The Second Coming* William Butler Yeats warned of a time when "the best lack all conviction, while the worst are full of passionate intensity." The life we have lost in the living is the life of wisdom, truth, and justice. We have lives of convenience and comfort, but we have lost character.

Moral education has fallen on hard times. The knowledge explosion has resulted in a fallout of ignorance. In *The Closing of the American Mind,* Allan Bloom, professor of social thought at the University of Chicago, laments "the disheartening expansion of trained ignorance and bad thought." For Bloom, "the university has become

[8]James T. Laney, "Education of the Heart," *Christianity Today*(February 6, 1987), p. 21.

society's conceptual warehouse of often harmful influences."[9] Students arrive at university ignorant of classical literature and music and resist a liberal arts education. They have no passion for real education, because they are absorbed in trivialities and fads.

According to Bloom, serious education has been circumvented by the premature ecstasies of rock music and sex. "The easy sex of teenagers snips the golden thread linking eros to education."[10] The search for truth is no longer respected, because relativism reigns as absolute and scientism and radical feminism combine in dissuading the student from exploring the thoughts and values of Western tradition. "Real religion and knowledge of the Bible have diminished to the vanishing point."[11] "The self is the modern substitute for the soul."[12] Graduates may be competent specialists and know how to market themselves well, but Bloom contends they are "flat-souled."[13] They are up-to-date, relevant, value-free, and conscious that they are determined by their economic success or failure, their sexual drives, and luck. In the depth of their being they are shallow. Like the emperor without his clothes, they parade in ignorance.

One day my son asked why Bloomington was chosen to be the site for Indiana University. His question made sense. Why would a major university make its home in the middle of rural Indiana, fifty miles from a major city? I presume that one reason for locating the university in a small town stemmed from a philosophy of education that sought to remove students from distractions and allow them to concentrate on the business at hand, which was gaining a worthwhile, well-rounded education. Times have

[9]Allan Bloom, *The Closing of the American Mind* (New York: Simon and Schuster, 1987), pp. 17–18.
[10]Ibid., p. 134.
[11]Ibid., p. 56.
[12]Ibid., p. 173.
[13]Ibid., p. 134.

changed, students come to university today looking for a good time, freedom, and hopefully a ticket to economic success.

Now the campus is a place of distractions—the more the better. If any proof is required, one need only walk through a co-ed dorm on an average school night. Education like almost everything else has become a consumer product to be gained with the least amount of cost and the greatest amount of pleasure. The university no longer lives up to its name, a community of scholars who recognize the ultimate unity of all truth and who pursue that truth with devotion. The moral as well as intellectual perception that all truth is God's truth has vanished, leaving in its absence the pressure of the market, the military-industrial complex, various interest groups, and whatever "wags-the-tail" to determine where the educational consumer mall will put its resources.

In Church

There is a lack of moral character in the church as well as in the culture. More attention has been given to religious externals and sentiment than to the cultivation of moral courage and conviction. If people are ignorant of the Bible they are also ignorant of a biblical morality. Perhaps the most evident sign of this moral demise is the loss of authentic Christian practice among second- and third-generation Christians who were never nurtured in the moral seriousness of true spirituality. Christianity impressed them as a religious game people play with little effect on their daily lives. Years of religious indoctrination and entertainment have resulted in a trained incapacity to think and act morally. Moral character has not been a priority.

Let me explain what I mean by character. Sometimes you hear people referring to a house as having character. It is usually an older home with a certain look and feel. The stone chimney, the wood trim, the colonial shutters, the swing on the veranda give the house "character." We all know certain unique, frequently witty, slightly eccentric people we call "real characters." I am not referring to character in this descriptive, superficial sense. What I mean by character is the quality of life we have lost in our increasingly secularized, self-centered way of living.

Character is the quality of being that applies moral attributes to everyday living. Not to be confused with personality, character is a matter of the heart that relates the deep aspirations for justice and righteousness to every dimension of our involvement in the world. Character formation through prayer and worship is the process of internalizing the wisdom and discernment we need in order to live as we ought to live. One of the great issues before us is whether the quality of our spirituality and ethical sensitivity nurtured in our churches is sufficient to develop true moral character.

Witness the large-scale retreat from serious thinking and the almost universal appeal of style and personality over substance and character. The scandals of a few church leaders are sensationalized, but the widespread insensitivity and moral immaturity of the church are ignored. Nowhere, it seems, is the personality cult more evident, and emotional slogans more popular, than in the church.

Many people come to church looking for an emotional lift and black-and-white answers. "Felt-needs" have little to do with discerning between good and evil but a lot to do with feeling good about yourself. "If Christians cannot communicate as thinking beings," writes Harry Blamires, "they are reduced to encountering one another only at the shallow level of gossip and small talk."[14]

Moral perspectives in the church vacillate between everyone doing what is right in their own eyes and everyone being told how to think. Money, power, leisure, business, and the environment are among the ethical issues left to personal opinion and private discretion by funda-

[14]Harry Blamires, *The Christian Mind* (London: SPCK, 1963), p. 13.

mentalists. Accountability in this realm is considered meddling. But on the subjects of abortion, nationalism, education, pornography, and sexual conduct conservative Christians are told by their leaders how to think and act.

Mainline Protestants tend to reverse the issues, preferring to focus on the evils of nuclear weapons, multinational corporations, racism, the poor, and the homeless. Personal morality, especially in the area of sexuality, is frequently left to cultural trends. Thus pornography is wrong, according to liberal church-bodies, not because it appeals to lust, but because it is sexist. Homosexuality, no longer the evil it was thought to be, now deserves acceptance as an alternative lifestyle. The religious moralism of either the right or the left must not be confused with moral character shaped by the Word and Spirit of God.

It is strange that Christians in some circles should find the word *ethics* talked about more in the culture than in the church. When ethics is mentioned, it is in reference to lying, stealing, cheating, and sex, as if this short list of "don'ts" exhausts the ethical challenge of the Christian. The word *justice* is synonymous with judgment not righteousness and is perceived in popular religious sentiment to have more to do with "law and order" than the Old Testament command for a just and equitable distribution of resources. The reaction against the "social gospel" has been so unthinking that much of the social ethic of the Bible has been ignored and replaced with a truncated form of evangelism unacquainted with Jesus' kingdom ethic.

Theoretically, as we might expect, the church highly favors moral character. Practically speaking, however, there is little time or energy for moral-order thinking and the education of the heart. Priority has been given to making people feel good about themselves, either because they are enlightened with the "new morality" or because they pride themselves on escaping the clutches of "worldliness." For the most part their "secular" professions are far removed from the implications of their religious faith, about as far removed as academic disciplines are from the principle that all truth is God's truth.

Moral-Order Thinking

Sweeping moral trends, revealed on camera, on campus, or in the church, depict a culture swaying between moralistic self-righteousness and relativistic self-pleasure. Neither extreme captures the meaning and purpose of the educated heart. Not only are we as a culture confused over what is morally right and wrong, but we have also lost our bearings on the moral purpose of life itself.

Morality is not simply a sequence of independent choices to which we respond either morally or immorally. The scope of morality embraces the totality of life. It encompasses the structure of family life, the preparation and purposes of vocation, the stewardship of resources, respect for the environment, and the pursuit of justice. It involves knowing how to suffer and how to comfort the suffering. It means living today in light of eternity and preparing for a good death. Morality concerns our motives and ambitions, our hopes and dreams. Morality is what the Bible calls righteousness and righteousness is what God determines is right.

The study of ethics does not begin with a study of issues, it begins with our heartfelt comprehension of God's moral order. Not too long ago I taught a course in moral medicine. The reaction of one of the medical doctors attending the seminar was fairly typical of how we generally think about morality. He claimed that 99 percent of the time he goes about doing surgery and meeting the needs of his patients without ever facing a moral issue. He had concluded that medical ethics was limited to controversial issues like abortion, euthanasia, genetic engineering, surrogate motherhood, etc. What he did not realize was that everything about medicine involves morality: our view of science and nature, the role of the servant-physician, the ethos of the medical profession, the purposes of technology, the accessibility of health care, the responsibilities of the patient, ministering to the dying and comforting the living.

Nor did he realize that the Christian physician may make many moral decisions on controversial issues like abortion and euthanasia, yet destroy the moral order of his profession by treating the disease and not the patient, by serving himself and not society, and by trusting in his own self-sufficiency.

Moral-order thinking applies to everything from medicine to merchandising and from parenting to publishing. It encompasses our deepest thoughts and our most obvious actions. That is why I have chosen to speak of educating the heart. The heart symbolizes who we are in the depth of our being. What we are outwardly may be a charade. The real issue is a man or woman's heart, which has a way of showing its true colors under the pressure of time and circumstance.

I hope that my referring to the heart will not cause confusion. A professor of insurance, who has spent a career honing the art of precise prose, said to me that he found the term "educating the heart" confusing and misleading. He did not see what the physical organ or an expression of sentiment had to do with ethics. My intention is to use the metaphor of the heart, an important biblical and cultural metaphor, to capture the essence of true ethical sensitivity, which is the product of God's grace and authentic human willingness.

An educated heart is informed and transformed by the Spirit of God; it embraces the affections as well as the mind, revealing in word and action through patient endurance authentic Christian character. Educating the heart is synonymous with being "thoroughly equipped for every good work" (2 Timothy 3:17). It involves becoming wise for salvation and being trained in all righteousness. Educating the heart involves a deep-seated internalization of moral-order character.

We need not make the "heart" into a mystery. I could

have chosen a more abstract expression, like the "depth of being" or the "essential self," but such phrases strike me as theoretical and impersonal. The heart is an uncontested biblical and cultural metaphor for who we are and who we are becoming. I have sent many cards and letters over the years to my wife affirming my love for her "with all my heart." Never once has Ginny sent the letter back with "heart" circled and a question mark added, wondering what I meant by "all my heart."

The apostle Paul's prayer for the servants of Christ at Philippi reminds us that moral discernment and action are the consequences of genuine love. It is a matter of the heart. "This is my prayer: that your love may abound more and more in knowledge and depth of insight, so that you may be able to discern what is best and may be pure and blameless until the day of Christ, filled with the fruit of righteousness that comes through Jesus Christ—to the glory and praise of God" (Phil. 1:9–11). True spirituality makes Christian ethics inseparable from authentic love. The choices of the heart proceed from an education motivated by love and abounding more and more in knowledge and depth of insight.

QUESTIONS FOR DISCUSSION

1. If life is so easy, why do we find living so difficult?
2. Do you believe that North American culture is facing a moral crisis?
3. Why is religion inadequate in coping with the present moral challenge?
4. Why are we as a culture not more concerned with the erosion of moral values?
5. If students are getting high marks academically, why are they having trouble with ordinary life?
6. Do you agree that our culture overemphasizes style, image, and personal pleasure?
7. Do you agree that a person's character is the starting point for ethical reflection and decision making?
8. What is involved in moral-order thinking?

2

A Divided Heart

Now if selves are defined by their preferences, but those preferences are arbitrary, then each self constitutes its own moral universe, and there is finally no way to reconcile conflicting claims about what is good in itself.
Robert Bellah, *Habits of the Heart*

An educated heart unites what the habits of the heart divide. Left to ourselves and our natural tendencies, we pursue a lifestyle that jeopardizes moral character and true spirituality for the sake of personal gratification, comfort, and self-fulfillment. It matters not whether the lifestyle is customized with the best the culture has to offer or vulgarized with all that is bad.

The individual self composes his or her own morality. In the extreme, the imperial self seeks for sensuality without love, intimacy without commitment, success without service, and expertise without wisdom. "Self-indulgence up to the very limits imposed by hygiene and economics" is a line from Aldous Huxley that well describes the habits of the heart under the uninhibited rule of self.[1]

For the majority, however, a self-determined morality is more modest. They have created their own criteria for "making it" in this world. It may be careerism or it may be successful family life. It may be working toward social reform or the freedom to travel. What is significant is that their goals are based on their radical individualism. They have concluded that they have a natural right to follow their own inclinations, predispositions, and intuitions. There is no moral imperative or inherent moral authority holding them accountable. As long as everyone does what is right in their own eyes and does not interfere with the self-fulfillment of others, everyone gets along fine.

In *Habits of the Heart*, Robert Bellah and a team of social analysts explore how Americans in the eighties approached the pursuit of happiness. In conversations with over two hundred Americans, they found a strong commitment to personal success achieved by individual choice and dependent on economic progress. They found that freedom was highly valued and meant "being left alone by others, not having other people's values, ideas, or styles of life forced upon one."[2] They concluded that Americans tend to think of justice "as a matter of equal opportunities for every individual to pursue whatever he or she understands by happiness."[3]

Individualism dominates the American persona and conditions the heart to pursue goals that jeopardize the moral life. As the authors of *Habits of the Heart* indicate, there is little thought among Americans about how the freedom to pursue economic success is related to our ultimate success as persons. Nor is much thought given to our failing capacity for commitment to others, because we

---

[1]Aldous Huxley, *Brave New World* (London: Granada, 1977), p. 190.
[2]Bellah, *Habits of the Heart*(New York: Harper & Row, 1985), p. 23.
[3]Ibid., p. 25.

have emphasized individual freedom to the point that "it becomes hard to forge bonds of attachment to, or cooperation with, other people, since such bonds would imply obligations that necessarily impinge on one's freedom."[4] It is a freedom "from the demands of conformity to family, friends, or community." But little is understood about the positive value of this freedom beyond that of individual independence. Therefore, in some sense the "freedom to be left alone is a freedom that implies being alone."[5]

The habits of the heart reflect the ethos of the American culture. It is sobering to realize that the American experience can be described accurately by popular commitments to radical individualism, personal ambition, consumerism, technological control, and sexual pleasure. These "first principles" have become ends in themselves unguided by a qualifying moral standard. Therefore they emerge within our culture as a "moral" force in their own right and shape a new standard of thought and conduct.

The word *ethics* is derived from the Greek word *ethos*, which means habit or custom. The development of modern ethics is more in keeping with the derivation of the word than is the ancient tradition of Christian theology that founded ethics on God's unchanging, eternally relevant moral wisdom. Today's ethos, with its accent on utilitarian and expressive individualism, conditions behavior to a new standard of success, freedom, and self-fulfillment.

I believe the habits of the heart are radically opposed to educating the heart. I have chosen the latter term to express the process of cultivation and nurture needed to resist willful compliance with cultural mores that are no longer biblically moral or truly life-fulfilling. At first there may appear to be little outward difference between the habits of the heart and the educated heart because we are living on the borrowed legacy of a Christian moral outlook. In time, however, those who live according to the habits of

[4]Ibid., p. 23.
[5]Ibid., p. 23.

the heart will be deemed more open-minded and liberated. They will be judged more worthy of respect than those who hold to what is deemed an archaic moral pretentiousness. Morality will be selectively turned upside down; not all positions on moral issues will change, but the fundamental foundation for morality will be transferred from God to the individual, self-centered self.

The tendency of the habits of the heart is to divide love from the commitment of marriage, leisure from spiritual rest, labor from a vocational calling, and personal satisfaction from the public good. This development will not be feared, but for the most part welcomed as essential to our newly defined "freedom."

Christian Immorality

We no longer agree together on what is moral and immoral. Previous generations experienced a greater moral consensus than we do today. There was a cultural accommodation to a Judeo-Christian heritage resulting in a common tradition of what was right and wrong. However, that shared moral understanding has crumbled, broken under the impact of the sexual and biomedical revolutions, the persistent influence of secularism and radical pluralism, fascination with mysticism and the occult and the widespread demise of a recognizable moral authority in North American culture. Therefore we have come to trust our feelings, our technology, our ambitions, and our self-interests more than a moral heritage even remotely connected to the Word of God.

What used to be moral is now found to be immoral by those who pride themselves on their progressive morality. In Roman times the early Christians were condemned as atheists because they refused to pay homage to the imperial cult. Their commitment to Jesus Christ alone as Lord and King brought the charge of undermining the ethos of the empire. They challenged the deification of Caesar and the sacralization of culture. It is ironic that Christians should be condemned as atheists when their goal was to confess "Jesus is Lord" in their personal as well as public lives. Today's charge is no less ironic. Christians are faced with the growing charge of immorality.

There are of course immoral ways of opposing abortion, propagating the Gospel, challenging genetic engineering, and working for justice among the poor, but that is not what I mean. The charge of immorality will be leveled against the Christian because he or she opposes the morality of the age.

Following the habits of heart, the morality of the age enshrines relativism and selfism as the ethical absolutes. The old ethic is not thrown out entirely. Popular morality still forbids such things as stealing, blackmail, insider trading on Wall Street, drug trafficking, and bribery. These acts are widely recognized as offensive and socially unworkable. But added to this old morality is a new ethic that approves of divorce on grounds of incompatibility and convenience, accepts abortion if the mother wishes, supports fetal tissue research if it will enhance health, encourages around-the-clock commerce seven days a week to improve the economy, approves of homosexual marriages, promotes death-induction, uses conspicuous material consumption as a sign of career success, backs mandatory genetic screening for genetic diseases and deformities, safeguards anonymity for the patient with infectious AIDS, condones sexual promiscuity, and pushes state-sponsored gambling—all, of course, in the name of enlightened freedom.

Public morality finds itself in opposition to Christian thinking and action. The Buffalo School District in New York State has filed a lawsuit against three high school students, because they met to have a Bible study when other student clubs met at McKinley High School. Although McKinley High allowed a Dungeons and Dragons group that focused on the occult, it would not permit a Bible-study group. The Christian Legal Society agreed to defend the three students against the Buffalo school board.

It is difficult to understand why the school board chose to waste its time and financial resources by filing a lawsuit against three of its students, when the plain intent of the Equal Access Act passed by Congress in 1984 protects this type of student-initiated and student-led religious meeting. Obviously some people are determined to see this action as illegal, if not immoral.

It has become apparent that our culture approaches morality from principles that render Christian action immoral. Values have been divorced from moral absolutes and are now the product of personal preference and social trends. In a seriously misguided and intentionally twisted view of the separation of church and state, public policy must now disavow absolutely all connection with biblical commands and understanding—an interpretation of the Constitution unthinkable to its original subscribers.

Joseph Fletcher, a well-known American ethicist and long-time proponent of this moral reversal, argues that we have eaten of the tree of knowledge and made ourselves like God. According to Fletcher, this act was one of freedom, not disobedience, because now the responsibility for our destiny lies with us. The age of innocence is over and the God who would limit our activity by moral "nevers" is only a doomed idol. Fletcher commends a "choice" ethic that encourages us to decide whether the baby in the womb is a disease or a person; enables us to select the genetic endowment of our offspring, ending "reproductive roulette"; and permits us to determine when to die. We create morality, Fletcher argues, by choosing rather than submitting. There are no moral nevers, he claims, no absolutes or binding precepts. If a baby is born against the choice of the mother, the child is not only unwanted but immoral.[6]

[6]Joseph Fletcher, "Technological Devices in Medical Care," in Stephen Lammers and Allen Verhey eds., On Moral Medicine (Grand Rapids: Eerdmans, 1987), pp. 220–27.

Religious Moralism

Ethics would be made much easier if there were a neat division between moral-order thinking and moral relativism, but that is not the case. The choice is not simply between a cultural morality and a church morality, between a secular ethic and a religious ethic.

The habits of the heart are the inherent product of the conditioned self rather than the commanded self. Cultural conditioning (whether it be relativistic or moralistic) runs counter to God's moral authority and ethical sensitivity. This may be a difficult concept to grasp, but the implications are obvious enough in our moral behavior. I am suggesting that from a biblical perspective hedonism and self-righteousness are much the same in God's eyes. It is no better to be a legalist than a relativist. Both perversions express a willful selfism that neglects the heart of God's commands and the meaning of biblical morality.

Moralistic thinking is the confusion of personal opinion and pat answers. It is the legalistic product of reactionary cultural trends and an external code of conduct. It is a group ethic shaped by peer pressure, cultural pride, and indoctrination. Moralistic attitudes are highly selective and frequently arbitrary in determining what is evil. And the proposed means for fighting such evil is as dehumanizing and unrighteous as the evil itself. The problem with moralistic thinking is that it divorces the inner character of the person from the unity of the moral universe. Therefore compliance with a moralistic ethic tends to be a matter of religious appearances and self-righteous attitudes. One is reminded of Aleksandr Solzhenitsyn's dictum "Life organized legalistically cannot defend itself against evil." It is this vulnerability to evil that results in the moralist's chief problem, namely, *fear*. The moralist is both defensive and defenseless.

The religious party of the Pharisees, during the time of Jesus, offers a case study in moralistic thinking. Ironically most of the opposition Jesus faced was not pagan but religious. The meaning of morality was at the heart of their dispute. The Pharisees advocated a precise and carefully nuanced interpretation of biblical law. Their aim was to apply the law in every conceivable situation. In time they added to the biblical commands a tradition of bylaws and applications designed to ensure an exacting program of righteousness.

It is not difficult to understand why attention shifted from the fundamental concerns of justice, mercy, and faithfulness to the specific details of dietary laws, tithing codes, and Sabbath rules. Obedience was reduced to a measurable performance test. Their zeal for the finer points of the law resulted in the formation of small communities dedicated to preserving their ceremonial purity and tithing obligations. Jesus was a threat to this approach to ethics. He was concerned with divorce, lust, anger, power, wealth, revenge, and lying. The Pharisees were concerned with tithing their spices, keeping up their image, and preserving their national identity. Jesus explored the heart; the Pharisees judged on appearances.

Moralistic thinking is as popular today as ever. I am convinced that just about every local church suffers the cancer of moralism. It is a form of oppression that quenches the church's spiritual vitality and moral wisdom. When the church needs to prayerfully and thoughtfully consider the whole counsel of God on moral issues, we have fervent advocates of a simplistic, pro-America, pro-family, pro-life, pro-military, pro-capitalist morality. I am sure that some Christians would feel it was heaven on earth if we could just return to the fifties, while another generation would think the same of the pre-twenties.

When I think of the religious moralist, I have in mind a person who holds the Bible in high honor, but whose understanding of the Bible is shaped by a rigid tradition of legalistic and literalistic piety. Frequently such a person has never been exposed to any other thinking about the Bible than what he or she has received from a small enclave of pastors, speakers and writers who are either poorly educated or narrowly educated and perpetuate their antipathy to education among their parishioners. They are as sincere and pious as the Pharisees and share their sense of group identity. They are worried about building a hedge around the truth and their children to protect against compromise; but ironically they end up denying the truth after the manner of the Pharisees.

What I found in America's heartland was a moralistic mentality, as damaging to a Christian ethic in the long run, as an openly immoral paganism. The very mentality that some people hope will block America's moral decline is in fact hastening it by producing a generation with the outward form and appearance of godliness but without moral character and courage. The moral, intellectual, and spiritual power of Jesus' ethic is denied. Eugene Peterson describes a common phenomenon:

> The church attracts to itself persons who like to live in the atmosphere of the holy but have little interest in being holy themselves. They find delight in working on committees and find security in ordering their lives within the reassuring traditions of the fathers. They are faithful in showing up in church on Sundays and are fortified by listening to the moral instruction of their leaders. But they have no appetite for holiness, or joy, or love.[7]

I will leave it to the reader to judge whether the series of "snapshots" below describes the religious moralist accurately or is an unfair caricature.

The religious moralist is very concerned to maintain a literal, six twenty-four-hour-day interpretation of the creation account but is equally unconcerned to develop and support a Christian environmental ethic.

The moralist sees no contradiction between supporting a "first-strike" nuclear arms policy and championing the

[7]Eugene Peterson, *Reversed Thunder: The Revelation of John and the Praying Imagination* (San Francisco: Harper & Row, 1988), pp. 51–52.

cause of world evangelism. Prayer is offered for our persecuted brothers and sisters living in Russia and China, while approval is given for aiming at them weapons of unimaginable destruction. Preserving our national interests seems more important than the life of the church in these countries.

Moralists insist on using the King James Version of the Bible for themselves and their children because they are suspicious of "modern" versions; yet they support missionaries who translate the Greek text of the New Testament into the vernacular of tribal dialects.

Like the Pharisees they think of stewardship in terms of a percentage of income. The rest of their resources belongs to them to do with as they please. If they have been so good as to give a tenth of the income to "the Lord's work," no matter how great their income may be, they are free to spend the rest on luxury cars, exotic vacations, and opulent homes. Somehow "the Lord's work" is more easily recognized in a television "ministry" than in personal contact with the poor in their home community or in financial support for a widow in their church.

Moralists believe they are upholding the sanctity of marriage by taking a hard line against all who have been divorced. Everyone who has been divorced for whatever reason is guilty and in many cases ostracized. Defending marriage is best served by a "don't bother me with the facts" attitude toward the grounds of divorce and biblical teaching.

Little preparation goes into the work of marriage. Much more attention is given to the wedding party's formal wear than to the meaning of the vows. And there is greater fuss and expense for the reception after the wedding than for the teaching and training before marriage. Schools are condemned for teaching classes in "sex education," but Sunday schools avoid the subject. A Bible class on a theology of sexuality offends some moralists as being too worldly.

There is considerable talk among moralists about

authority and the "chain of command." Headship belongs to the male, irrespective of his capability for moral leadership and spiritual discernment. Spiritually minded women are passed over for service in the church while ego-driven males are placed in positions of leadership. Both male and female moralists deny women a significant role in ministry, claiming that the apostle Paul's handling of situational problems in Corinth or Ephesus is absolutely normative for every local church, regardless of whether the specific problem is male chauvinism or radical egalitarianism.

Moralists relate to the global church in terms of white missionaries and their native prodigies. Their missionaries may be sensitive and responsive to cross-cultural dynamics, free of most of the prejudices popular in the bygone era of colonialism, but for themselves they ignore the dynamic and vitality of the indigenous church. They consider their own version of Christianity more developed and more mature than anything that could be happening in the so-called Third World.

The moralist is leery of social justice issues because he associates them with the so-called social gospel and the liberal political agenda. Concern for the homeless, the poor, and the unemployed are seen as a diversion from the main business at hand, "telling people about Jesus." Abortion and pornography are notable exceptions, but the comprehensiveness of Jesus' kingdom ethic remains a foreign concept.

Most moralists cannot conceive of a genuine Christian being anything other than a pretribulation rapture dispensationalist. They claim that to interpret the book of Revelation differently denies a literal reading of God's Word. Such Christians expect to be spared the dire persecution reported in the Apocalypse. Since the world is coming to an end, the work of the church should concentrate on "life-boat" evangelism. Since the culture is growing more and more decadent, there is little point in working for long-term social reform. However, the decadence and depravity of the world do not dissuade them from entrepreneurial excitement in the free enterprise system.

Interracial marriages are frowned upon by moralists because "Christians should not be unequally yoked." They claim that such marriages are unnatural. Discrimination persists against American blacks, though large amounts of money are given to evangelize African blacks.

Champions of patriotism and the Declaration of Independence, moralists have a history of condemning minorities. They opposed the civil-rights movement of the sixties by slandering Martin Luther King, Jr. and other leaders as communist sympathizers. Now they condemn advocates for justice in South Africa, such as Desmond Tutu and Allan Boesak, as anarchists. Americans celebrate a war over taxation without representation as an act of moral courage but denounce Christians in their struggle against apartheid.

More "snapshots" could be added to this collection depicting the moralist, but the picture of a divided heart is already clear. Externally there is a commitment to biblical authority, but in actual fact the Bible is frequently interpreted carelessly and thoughtlessly. The commands of God are treated selectively; in some cases they are exaggerated, in other cases they are ignored. The power of cultural and religious conditioning results in an ethical insensitivity and moral laxity evident to everyone but the moralist himself. No wonder Jesus found the righteousness of the Pharisees intolerable and considered them worse off than those who were blatantly immoral.

We have sadly failed to distinguish between the religiously and culturally conditioned habits of the heart and the heart truly educated in the moral character of God and his Word. How do we distinguish between personal opinion and biblical conviction? What is the difference between indoctrination and education? Does the government have a responsibility to preserve moral order through legislation and enforcement or are all laws that require moral behavior moralistic? One of my objectives in this study is to answer these questions and clarify the differences between these two approaches to ethics. One of the most important issues in Christian ethics should be to distinguish between a pharisaical and legalistic moralism and a moral-order ethic that takes its lead from Jesus and the apostles.

Moral Confusion

We will continue in moral confusion if we insist that there are only two ethical categories to choose from, namely, relativism and moralism. Both of these ethical approaches are immoral and are motivated by pride and fear; both express the habits of the heart untutored in the will of God; both fail to recognize the nature of true moral-order thinking.

One of the reasons for the popularity of moral relativism is its resistance to moralistic thinking. It is a defense against the self-righteous pride of religiously defended prejudice and moral apathy. Many fear the so-called puritanical tyranny that threatens society if moralizers impose their will on culture the way they would like to.

The roots of relativism have been sunk deep into our cultural ethos. Western civilization has undergone a profound rejection of moral authority. As a culture we have lost faith in God and the authority of the Author of life to guide our personal goals and public actions. Portraying the American dream has meant leaving God out of the picture and refashioning morality to suit our comfort zones and coping strategies. It has served the purpose of popular morality, which extols the virtues of personal freedom, material success, and self-indulgence and ignores the difference between empty moralism and biblical morality.

In the mind of many there is just no such distinction, and therein lies the fundamental confusion. All morality has become legalism. Moral authority is disparaged in any form as an intrusion on the free spirit of the liberated modern man and woman. Society is made up of individuals governed by the dictates of their own hearts. Personal values are legitimate as long as they do not intrude on another person's freedom. Personal preference becomes the chief criterion for an individualized code of ethics. Everyone does what is right in his or her own eyes.

By contrast, moral-order thinking is the character and conviction of the heart guided by the Author of life. The purpose of our study is to offer an alternative to the habits of the heart, whether they be religious habits or secular habits. Moral-order thinking unites what the divided heart casts off. True spirituality and true humanness are not divorced. Humility graces an ethical responsiveness that seeks through the power of prayer and patient endurance, righteousness and justice in an evil world. Character is shaped from the inside out by the Word and Spirit of God. It is a work of grace not law, a matter of choice not coercion. Moral-order thinking does not depend on group enthusiasm or the zeal of an admiring audience, yet true moral conviction gains strength in community. It is a personal faith with public impact not a private faith with public rhetoric. Moral-order thinking affords a humble freedom to live for God, not religion, in a world apart from God. Obedience to the moral-order ethic is a matter of the heart.

Instant Morality

Choosing between the habits of the heart and the educated heart means rejecting ethical relativism *and* ethical moralism. It is the first order of business for ethics. But making it first does not make it easy or elementary. Choosing between popular trends and true precepts requires discernment. Wisdom is needed to move beyond our personal comfort zones of permissiveness and legalism.

In Huxley's *Brave New World* the Controller explains to the Savage, "There's no such thing as a divided allegiance; you're so conditioned that you can't help doing what you ought to do." And just in case something unpleasant should arise a pill is provided, labeled *soma*—designed "to give you a holiday from the facts." In Huxley's futuristic civilization, which had chosen machinery, medicine, and universal happiness instead of God, there was always *soma* "to calm your anger, to reconcile you to your enemies, to make you patient and long-suffering." The Controller praises the drug's benefits:

> In the past you could only accomplish these things by making a great effort and after years of hard moral training. Now, you swallow two or three half-gramme tablets, and there you are. Anybody can be virtuous now. You can carry at least half your morality about in a bottle. Christianity without tears—that's what *soma* is."[8]

We may wish for a Christianity without tears but it would certainly not be authentic Christianity. It may be religious, complete with Sunday services and doctrine but it would fail to please Christ. There is no instant morality. Even a sincere conversion from unbelief to commitment to Jesus Christ does not produce an educated heart overnight. Nothing can replace the hard work of moral training. Ethical sensitivity needs to be nurtured and developed. The deceptiveness of sin needs to be exposed and the lessons of moral pain learned in the crucible of life. That is why the followers of Christ have been given the Holy Spirit to guide them in all truth. But Jesus never promised an automatic, painless process.

QUESTIONS FOR DISCUSSION

1. Do you agree that the ultimate moral authority for many Americans is themselves?
2. How would you describe the morality of the age?

[8]Huxley, *Brave New World*, p. 190.

3. What important qualities are divorced in a divided heart?
4. Do you believe that Christian moral convictions may eventually be labeled immoral?
5. Do you agree that moralistic thinking is as dangerous to the development of moral character as relativistic thinking?
6. Do you think that the moralistic mentality described in this chapter is a pressing issue for the North American church?
7. How has your family and church experience prepared you for moral-order living?

3

The Art of Living

> *He was going to do something—something star-*
> *tling, something rash, something desperate, what-*
> *ever it took. He was going to break out of here. He*
> *was going to rise up from this muck. He was going*
> *to light up the sky, seize the Life for himself.*
> Tom Wolfe, *The Bonfire of the Vanities*

At the corner of Bloor and Avenue Road in Toronto
there is a sign just before the Church of the Redeemer that
reads "Discover the Art of Living." As one walks west on
Bloor, it appears to be a sign for the church. It is not. It is
an advertisement for a new luxury condominium being
built next door. The sign captures the wisdom of the age:
The art of living is knowing *where* to live—in a luxury
"condo"—not *how* to live.

Conventional Wisdom

Contrary to popular opinion, the art of living cannot
be pictured in home decorating magazines or discovered on

talk shows. Obviously we will have to go beyond trivial sources if we want to know what life is all about. "Lifestyle" magazines do not tell us how to live. They tell us how to play. If we want to know how to live we will have to choose the life we have lost in the living. We will have to choose the obedient self over the techniques of self-management. The habits of the heart reduce ethics to a personal style. Life is decorated according to the behavioral customs of Pharisee or Philistine.

A true artist uses his or her medium of expression with integrity. Creativity takes place within the context of truth. The trained musician is obedient to the score. The experienced painter understands the characteristics of watercolors or oil. The successful sculptor knows how to fashion a statue out of stone because he has learned to appreciate the qualities of marble. Moral and spiritual life is to human beings what the body is to the physician or what steel, concrete, and glass are to the architect. We must choose to respond to life according to its own integrity.

If we want to get the most out of life we have to understand what life is all about. The art of living requires the practical and personal acknowledgment that we are moral, spiritual beings made in the image of God. Personhood is not the product of time plus chance. Life is not reducible to the DNA molecule. Works of art are a testimony to the artist just as life is a testimony to our Creator. The reason people will pay $53.9 million for a painting is not that they want an oil painting of *Irises* hanging on their wall. They want to invest in a work by Van Gogh.

Faith is the essential human investment in God. It is the reasoned conviction that the cosmos is the result of God's action and revelation. We are not cosmic orphans. "By faith we understand that the universe was formed at God's command," wrote the author of Hebrews, "so that what is seen was not made out of what was visible" (Heb. 11:3).

Faith takes us beyond scientific proofs and philosophical speculations and allows us to live our lives according to the Word of God rather than the latest word of science or philosophy. Faith does not diminish the importance of science and philosophy. On the contrary, faith provides for these disciplines by declaring their purposefulness in a universe endowed by its Creator with meaning and personhood. The scientist and philosopher can approach their work with the conviction that their own worth and the worthiness of their profession is assured in a moral, rather than a mechanistic universe. Faith challenges the idolatry of science and philosophy and encourages their free exercise according to a true understanding of the universe.

According to the wisdom of the age, the art of living is making a living. It is knowing where to live not how to live. It is looking out for number one and keeping your options open. It is making a name for oneself and taking one day at a time. Conventional wisdom sells well in thirty-second spots on a 19-inch screen. It is not demanding, requires no critical thought, and appeals to our natural selves. It is a worldview reducible to commercials and one-liners.

A Modern Spirit

Absalom is a surprisingly contemporary figure for having lived nearly three thousand years ago! His story offers us a challenging case study in moral behavior with striking similarities to today's morality. You would think that the third son of Israel's King David might be of interest only to historians who like to note insignificant details. But ancient Absalom has a modern spirit about him. The habits of his heart remind us of our own.

The biblical story of Absalom (2 Sam. 13–18) covers about a decade of his life, probably from his early twenties into his thirties. It is an especially critical stage of life for most of us, when choices and decisions that bear lasting consequences are made. Born into privilege and power, Absalom wanted to decide his own destiny. He was unwilling to walk in his father's shadow. Absalom sought to make a name for himself and he coveted his father's power. Like so many today Absalom's life revolved around himself—his ambition, his pride, and his hate. He was determined to fulfill his self-appointed destiny.

His story begins with moral pain and outrage. From the start the choices of his heart seem determined by an evil beyond his power to prevent. It is this evil, which he did not choose, that will set the course of his life. Absalom did not look for trouble; it came his way unexpectedly, without request, forcing him to cope with an act and a person who hated what he loved.

Sadly this is where moral decision-making begins for many people. They have not chosen to be brought up in an atmosphere of substance abuse or infidelity or greed or prejudice, that is just how life has happened to them. Ethics for us all is not in the first instance a classroom lecture but a practical life question: How will we personally overcome the evil around us and in us? Absalom was either unwilling or incapable of coping with evil without committing evil. He had no other strategy than to fight evil with the weapons of bitterness and hate.

Absalom's stepbrother, Amnon, fell in love with Tamar, the beautiful sister of Absalom. Amnon became so frustrated in his infatuation over her that he became ill. All he could think about was Tamar and "it seemed impossible for him to do anything to her" (2 Sam. 13:2). Amnon's cousin Jonadab recognized that "look" and saw an opportunity to do some scheming. Whether or not he stood to gain personally is difficult to know. Some people simply enjoy shrewdly manipulating other people's lives. It gives them a sense of power. Amnon explained his dilemma, and Jonadab had a solution. "Pretend to be ill and when your father, the king, visits your bedside, let him know that a meal prepared and served by Tamar would be a big encouragement." The plan worked and Tamar was innocently sent into a situation prepared by deception and energized by lust.

Alone with Tamar, Amnon took advantage of the situation and grabbed her, forcing her onto his bed. It was a scene that is reenacted on prime-time television several times a night without a second thought from a generation exposed to Jonadab-style counsel and creativity. Tamar bravely sought to defend herself by a moral reasoning deeply felt in the conscience of God's people: "Such a thing should not be done in Israel! Don't do this wicked thing" (13:12).

Tamar understood this threat very differently from the majority of high school girls and university co-eds. Whether she had sex with Amnon willingly or unwillingly did not change the moral consequences of Amnon's actions. If Tamar had jumped into bed with Amnon willingly, caught up in the passion of the moment, the liaison would still have been wicked. The moral issue is not that Amnon violated her choice but that he violated her. Both fornication and rape are evil in God's sight.

The irony of our culture is that we approve of lust, pornography, and fornication and then turn around and condemn rape as if they are unrelated. Those who contend that rape is not a crime of passion but a crime of violence are making a deceptive and unnecessary distinction. Sexual morality is beautifully integrated and ordered in a fashion that does not allow us to condemn rape without also condemning premarital sex and adultery. A society that expects children in their early teens to become sexually active and proudly encourages sexual "freedom" should be prepared to sponsor many counseling centers for the victims of rape and incest.

Having used Tamar's body and fulfilled his lust, Amnon's passionate infatuation turns to hatred. He sends her away utterly humiliated and wasted as if he had done this wicked thing to an animal rather than to a person. Tamar expresses honestly and painfully the agony of her soul. Her moral wisdom preserved a painful sense of injustice. She has not been conditioned to respond in despair. She had been taught by her conscience and her community to feel the pain of immorality. Her own conscience and acquired moral insight accentuate the trauma. Her disgrace is not a cultural fiction or a figment of her imagination that can be remedied by psychological therapy. She must take this to heart, not because she is a woman, not because of cultural convention, not because she has been traumatized by a violent act, but because the command of God has been broken over her, against her, and in spite of her; that is why her heart is broken.

Shattered and distraught, Tamar sought the comfort and protection of her brother Absalom. He meant to console her but his obtuse and insensitive words denied her the empathy she so desperately needed: "Be quiet now, my sister; he is your brother. Don't take this thing to heart" (13:20). How could she *not* take this "thing" to heart? Absalom cannot even mention the word "rape." He is the picture of self-control and emotional denial.

Absalom's attempt to calm Tamar's despair by belittling Amnon's evil served as a cover for his inner rage. Not only was Tamar a victim of evil but Absalom became a victim as well. Neither of them had the character to deal with the evil. Tamar, we are told, became "a desolate woman," and Absalom began to plot a strategy for getting even. Vengeance filled his heart as despair had broken hers. They appear to have had no other recourse than despair and hate. Who can measure the powerful energy of hate that controls the choices of the heart?

David was furious when he heard the news. But he did nothing. His failure to act on behalf of justice exposed the weakness of his moral persuasion and lack of moral courage. His love for Amnon caused him to turn a blind eye to the tragedy of his daughter. David's silence revealed a guilty acquiescence to immorality and was directly responsible for Absalom's silent strategizing for revenge. Neither David nor Absalom knew how to face the evil with an honesty and integrity truly supportive of Tamar. Absalom's life became a picture of scheming, cutthroat competition. He may not have appeared to be adversarial, but in reality he was strategizing and plotting to have his own way from that point on.

Absalom's hatred was allowed to fester for two years before he set his trap for Amnon. And even then only the suspicion of malice lingered in the mind of David as Absalom urged the king to permit Amnon to attend his party. Absalom was a picture of complete self-control. He never betrayed his passion for revenge. His self-imposed code of silence prepared the way for him to strike. Convinced of the justice of his cause he lulled Amnon into a death trap and then fled to his wife's homeland in Geshur.

Ironically it was Jonadab who brought the news to David that Amnon had been killed by Absalom. In fact Jonadab, in his unflappable public relations style, made it sound like good news. Knowing that David feared a massacre of his many sons he quickly assured David that only Amnon had died. Calm and collected, Jonadab stood before the king explaining how this killing was "Absalom's expressed intention ever since the day Amnon raped his sister Tamar" (2 Sam. 13:32). Like many counselors before and after him, Jonadab was able to plant the seed of evil action without being held responsible (until the final judgment, that is).

Three years later Joab, the king's military commander, convinced David to allow his banished son to return to Jerusalem. The king stipulated that Absalom could return under the condition that he not see his face. Sometime during the three years in Geshur and the two years in Jerusalem Absalom's three sons died. It is likely that they died in infancy because their names are not given. Only his daughter's name is given and she is named after her Aunt Tamar.

We can only imagine the personal trauma of Absalom. His father refused to see him, and three of his four children had died. He must have been a desperately unhappy man, living for two years in Jerusalem under virtual house arrest. His frustration was compounded by Joab's refusal to respond to his summons; so he took a bold step to get

Joab's attention. He had Joab's barley field set on fire. Joab finally came to Absalom and received what sounded more like an ultimatum than a request.

Absalom challenged the moral courage of his father: "I want to see the king's face, and if I am guilty of anything, let him put me to death" (2 Sam. 14:32). Given David's moral feebleness, Absalom probably figured the risk was safe. If he was able to win Joab over through intimidation, why not confront the king and force the issue? Joab brought Absalom's message to the king, and David welcomed his son with a kiss and apparently a royal pardon.

A Master of the Universe

The story of Absalom does not end there. Out of the tragedy of his past, Absalom was prepared to forge ahead and create his own destiny. The habits of his heart had been shaped by vengeance and the struggle to survive. Now, he was ready to succeed by any means that would achieve his goals.

Absalom was a master at manipulating a situation in his favor. With his public disgrace overcome, Absalom began to climb the ladder of success and fixate on the throne the way Amnon had lusted after Tamar. He was a self-made man. He prided himself on his control; a real charmer, he knew when to be tough and when to let up. He saw himself on his father's throne and strategized to fulfill his self-appointed destiny.

We are told that Absalom "stole the hearts of the men of Israel" (2 Sam. 15:6). He was a man of appearances, reportedly the most handsome man in all of Israel and undoubtedly one of the best dressed. He knew the value of image-making and public relations. He surrounded himself with the symbols of power and success, including an escort of fifty men. Absalom positioned himself on the main road leading to the city gate so he could intercept his father's subjects. He promised them that if he were in power their rights would be defended. He was out to win them over. They came seeking justice and Absalom came seeking power. He was an opportunist who knew how to play on the emotions of sincere citizens who needed the king's counsel and action. Absalom made people feel important. He didn't care about justice. He used "justice" as part of his self-promotion.

After four years of embracing constituents, listening to complaints, and promising whatever people wanted, Absalom had stolen enough hearts to pull off his coup. The choices of his heart were self-serving. He had developed a following based on image and appearances. He was a master of deception, manipulation, and public relations, and his "style" of leadership had won them over. People were ready to risk their lives for his success. Absalom failed. But he came very close to pulling it off.

Today, Absalom-like strategies are firmly entrenched in the workplace, the church, and the home. Absalom the risk-taker, image-maker, public-relations expert, and power-player is a model for the ambitious man or woman who wants to make it in the real world. We have been sold the habits of the heart—the habits of hate, deception, selfishness, and power. The Bible's last word on Absalom describes his effort to leave a memorial to his name. Because he had no son, he erected a pillar in the King's Valley as a monument to himself. He named it after himself calling it, "Absalom's Monument" (18:18). The pillar is long gone, but a symbolic monument remains. Every time we choose the habits of the heart, we memorialize the name of Absalom.

Lost in the Living

The strategies of self-deception need to be comprehended and our own disobedience exposed. The moral pain we feel as a result of our own evil and the evil of others needs to be dealt with. We cannot acquire an educated heart without an earnest desire for it. True moral character cannot be expected apart from spiritual transformation, obedience to the whole counsel of God, and the earnest expectation of wise discernment. God forces neither salvation nor sanctification upon us. If the educated heart is not our desire, it will not be our experience.

It is a strange paradox that in an age of growing scientific, technological, military, political, and economic complexity men and women should be so complacent, content to live with such simplistic answers to our moral and spiritual crises. The art of living that advises "safe sex" rather than moral sex, measures a man by his income and a woman by her clothes, worships in the corporate cult, focuses on the body, and is more interested in counting calories than in the needs of others has forgotten the meaning of life. Such life denies the true meaning of living and is inclined to view God's commands as impertinent. The Author of life is ignored in the living, and we are the losers.

QUESTIONS FOR DISCUSSION

1. What makes life worth living?
2. Do you agree that the art of living requires the practical and personal acknowledgment that we are moral and spiritual beings made in God's image?
3. Why are many people attracted to fads and trends in morality?
4. How would you compare the human person made in God's image with the human person made in the media image?
5. Do you agree that ethics is not in the first instance an academic exercise but a practical life issue?
6. Why was Tamar so upset over Amnon's actions? How does her judgment of Amnon's actions differ from a contemporary assessment?
7. How should Absalom have responded to Tamar's experience?

8. How does the ancient example of Absalom portray the modern outlook?
9. How effective are the strategies of Absalom in our culture? Do you believe that Absalom's expressive individualism has a place in the Christian's life?

4

A Worn-out Morality

> *Train a child in the way he should go, and when he is old he will not turn from it.*
>
> Proverbs 22:6
>
> *It is part of the misguided and whimsical condition of humankind that we so devoutly believe in the power of effort-at-the-moment-of-action alone to accomplish what we want and completely ignore the need for character change in our lives as a whole.*
>
> Dallas Willard, *The Spirit of the Disciplines*

We learn a lot about ourselves by examining the past. I am intrigued by the emotional similarities between parents and their children. The carryover from one generation to another of personality traits is fascinating to observe. It is humorous to hear parents complain about their children's attitudes when they are almost the mirrored reflection of their own personality traits. Who we are as moral and spiritual beings has deep roots in our early moral training and our conditioning. Were we taught to think through the moral implications of our decisions or conditioned to fend for ourselves? Were those who sought justice commended in our families or condemned as troublemakers? Did we grow up appreciating the challenge our parents faced living Jesus' ethic on the job?

It makes sense for counselors to delve into our past to understand our emotional strengths and weaknesses. By talking about the significant relationships of our life with someone who is able to ask discerning questions and make insightful observations, we understand who we are and why we respond the way we do. What is true of our emotional outlook is also true of our ethical perspectives. Who we are as moral beings reflects a history of relationships, examples, teachings, and experiences. Just as we need to explore our roots to get our emotional bearings, we need to consider our past to discover the strengths and weaknesses of our moral maturity.

We need to examine our moral heritage and challenge the ideas and patterns that have shaped our ethical practice. Are we reactionary or righteous in our moral outlook? If we have been denied the example of true character and spiritual strength, we may be tempted to feel justified in doing our own thing. If we have rebelled against moralistic thinking, our tendency may be to throw out moral-order thinking and embrace relativism. By virtue of being victims of moral weakness and confusion we can unknowingly perpetuate evil.

For many Christians raised in a more "fundamentalist" background, moviegoing was a major compromise with worldliness and a direct, if not automatic, link to moral demise, particularly sexual immorality. The feeling was so strong that theaters were off-limits, even when the *Sound of Music* was playing. I believe this was more reactionary than it was righteous and illustrates the product of moralistic thinking. However, the pendulum has now swung in the opposite direction toward a thoughtless moral leniency. Christians have adapted comfortably to a steady diet of violence and sex in theaters and on television for the sake of passive entertainment. Many Christians thoroughly enjoy "comedies" filled with immoral innuendo and black humor with barely a tinge of moral sensitivity to what their parents would have found morally repulsive. "Worldliness" is not only *not* the problem it once was; it is now not the problem the apostle John thought it was when he wrote:

> Do not love the world or anything in the world. If anyone loves the world, the love of the Father is not in him. For everything in the world—the cravings of sinful man, the lust of his eyes and the boasting of what he has and does—comes not from the Father but from the world. (1 John 2:15–16)

A similar point may be made over the observance of the Sabbath rest. American Christians have grown so casual about the meaning of Sunday and the importance of worship that "services" are simply a break-in-the-action, sandwiched between sporting events, brunches, trips to the mall, camping, and a never-ending pursuit of leisure. It used to be that you couldn't play ball in the backyard on Sunday afternoon between a full morning in church and a good thirty minutes of biblical instruction Sunday evening. Now sporadic church attendance, one or two Sundays a month, even for the "faithful," is common practice. The problem is that we have dismissed an older generation's attitudes as being legalistic and moralistic, without the moral good sense and spiritual insight to grasp the meaning of a day apart for worship and spiritual renewal. I would venture to say that consistency in worship and continuity in the body-life of the Christian community are at an all-time low. On this issue, as well as others, many have easily passed from a moralistic narrowness to a cultural conformity without ever engaging in moral-order thinking.

As the two issues briefly mentioned above indicate, the formation of moral character requires serious attention.

We need to question our moral roots. Why do we hold the positions we do on abortion, success, nuclear war, sexuality, and poverty? How has our family and church background contributed to our ethical outlook? Are our moral roots in an ethic of convenience or in the wisdom of God? The roots of wisdom are important and should be identified.

Like Father, Like Son

Solomon and Absalom were sons of the same father. Through them we see the effectiveness and the failure of David's moral legacy. David played a major role in shaping the moral and spiritual direction of his two sons. Solomon's simple request for a discerning heart reminds us of David. We hear in Solomon's desire for an educated heart echoes of David's own prayers. But the influence of David is also apparent in the life of Absalom. Absalom's pursuit of power and prestige came as a reaction to the moral feebleness of his father. David's legacy was a mixed blessing. His moral strength inspired Solomon's desire for wisdom, but his moral weakness turned Absalom to foolishness.

In literature a minor character is often a foil for the major character. The contrast between characters helps us to better understand the leading character. When I go to an Indiana University basketball game I catch myself watching only "my" team and miss some of the most significant action in my narrowness. The other team serves only as a backdrop for the performance of the "home" team, and the event becomes less of a game.

The main "player" in the history surrounding Absalom is not Absalom but David, who is described by God as "a man after his own heart" (1 Sam. 13:14). David is to Absalom what the main player on the home team is to a second-string player on the visiting team. If Absalom were not David's son I imagine his life would be little more than a historical footnote. There are plenty of contemporary

"Absaloms," but David's son deserves special attention because he highlights an especially difficult time for his father. Absalom's life can teach us a great deal about the habits of the heart both in himself and in his father.

Surprised by Ethics

In the latter part of his reign David reminds me of many Christians who have grown weary with Christian living. They seem either surprised by, or oblivious to, the intensity of the spiritual and moral struggle that surrounds them. They have carried the "take life easy" philosophy into their homes and churches. They may have a zeal for evangelism but often they are ethically insensitive.

It is commonly thought among professing believers that witnessing has little to do with ethics. Sharing the Gospel and pursuing justice are considered very different. Each belongs in its own compartment of life. In the marketplace these spirit-weary Christians are bright, energetic, high achievers, but when it comes to Christ's lordship in the workplace, they seem bored and indifferent, unaware of the issues at stake. They remember a former zeal, perhaps during their student days, which has mellowed considerably with kids, mortgages, vacations, promotions, ailments, and material things. The difficulty with this mellowing process is that it is a compromise. Having lost their first love for Christ they drift away from wisdom to foolishness and from ethical sensitivity to moral leniency.

It is difficult to prepare a couple adequately for what parenting their first child will be like. It is hard to put into words the sleepless nights, the bane of colds and ear infections, the change of lifestyle, and the changing of diapers. Yet who can describe that overwhelming sense of love a parent feels for a child or put a price tag on the ecstatic greeting of a two-year-old as you walk through the back door after a trying day at work. However, if mothers and fathers were omniscient, they might have second thoughts about parenting; happily they are not. Some knowledge is good to acquire in small dosages with a great measure of humility. Parenting is a daily task with a lifelong commitment to love and nurture. It is a good analogy for the Christian life and the ongoing need to develop moral maturity.

I know one mother who is great with babies but indifferent toward any child two years and older. She loves the "baby-stage," the cuddling, feeding, fussing-over phase, but when the baby outgrows infancy she loses interest. This woman reminds me of those who love the "new birth" enthusiasm surrounding their initial conversion to Christ, only to find their gratitude and moral earnestness slipping away with the passing of years. Often they have never connected in their own minds the relationship between God's offer of salvation in Christ and daily, practical obedience to the kingdom ethic of Jesus. If they knew the ethic of the Cross they might have second thoughts about becoming a Christian in the first place.

Moral Energy

I am continually surprised by the energy required to be a Christian parent. There is no such thing as casual parenting. Children do not grow up into thinking, loving, caring human beings automatically. They need nurture, instruction, discipline, and example. After their conversion to Christ, they do not simply acquire an educated heart. They do not naturally become reflective Christians and doers of righteousness. My children need to see and feel my passion for holy living. They need both my discipline and my love. They need to know my struggles and weaknesses. They need to hear me ask for forgiveness and demand obedience. As I grow older and as I talk with older parents, I am learning that doing battle with the habits of the heart is never over. No matter how much energy we expend providing our children with middle-class comforts, we fail them and God if we become casual about their spiritual and moral development.

I am impressed by the energy it takes to think Christianly. How much easier it would be to pursue a career without reflection and discernment. It's discomforting to ask a lot of questions, to challenge motivations, to discern possible implications. Why not just accept the promotion without asking how it will affect my spiritual well-being and family life? Why go to all the trouble of challenging the marketplace mentality on competition, self-worth, and employee-employer relations? It would be a whole lot easier if we just did our work and didn't ask questions. So we are tempted to conform to the pressures of professionalism. We are inclined to go along with the customary way of doing things. We fail to consider that what we do may not agree with a Christian ethic.

I am also surprised at the energy it takes to belong to the Christian community as a servant rather than as a spectator. It would be much easier for me, when I consider the habits of my heart, to live unto myself and for myself. "I like to keep my weekends flexible," some say. "I don't like being tied down to a responsibility that requires a weekly commitment. It's important for me to get away for the weekend and create some space for myself. I have to get away from work and the phone."

Others say, "When I go to church Sunday morning I like to hear the good old hymns and a moving sermon that speaks to me where I am. It's important that our church be warm and friendly and I expect the pastor to be there when we need him. Yet when I go to church I feel artificial, like a plastic flower. Even my smile is part of my outfit. I resent the boredom." Perhaps we understand the difference between belonging to the biblical community as a servant and putting in an appearance as a spectator, but we have trouble changing.

Even the energy required to grow old as a Christian surprises me. In significant ways our culture is oriented around retirement. We invest and plan for the day when our number one *pre*occupation will be replaced by leisure. Old age means getting out of work and obligations and doing only what we want to do, when we want to do it. It means securing the future with health-care insurance, investments, and certificates of deposit. Retirement is supposedly a time of freedom. But for many it means loneliness, purposelessness, and an oversensitivity to their feelings. Educated professionals who have read nothing but newspapers and trade journals for forty years find little interest in reading. Those who have depended on the pressure of the workplace to set their priorities are suddenly left without motivation. Instead of reflection and service, retirees may become rigid in their ways or blindly uncritical of spiritual responsibility. Long before the mind and heart yield to aging, the will to strive for God's wisdom wanes.

The premium placed on youthfulness comes back to haunt us in our old age. Over the years we have fallen into the Absalom syndrome and substituted image for integrity, warmth in place of truth, congeniality in lieu of conscience, and style instead of substance. Ironically the youth culture dictates our self-perception, thus perpetuating moral imma- turity right up the scale from middle-aged professionals to elderly pensioners. When we have lost our physical energy and youthful vitality, we feel all used up, because we have bought the lie that "bio-strength" and sex appeal are more important than wisdom. We discover that we have failed to invest in wisdom the way we have invested in pensions and insurance. We lack the spiritual insight and moral energy to accept physical weakness and death. We have retired from building character the same way we have retired from the work force. We have little to say to our grandchildren about the moral challenges they face.

The energy required to grow old with the wisdom of God is tremendous, but few are willing to pay the price. We need retirees with a sense of God's call on their life and an earnest desire to fulfill their vocation. Their employment may cease but that certainly does not mean that their usefulness to the kingdom of God is over. The body of Christ, the church, would be enriched greatly if an older generation would take seriously the challenge of the educated heart.

Moral Failure

David's moral inheritance was a mixed blessing. The biblical portrait of David shows two sides to his character. One side exemplified moral courage and righteous action while the other side exposed moral weakness and injustice. The proportion of good to evil need not occupy our attention. He is described as a man after God's own heart. His passion for God, vividly expressed throughout the Psalms, cannot be challenged. There is no question that David bequeathed a rich spiritual legacy. But that makes it all the more difficult to explain his moral failure and weakness toward the end of his reign. Absalom was hurt by this other side of David's legacy. He was unable to cope with David's inability to act with moral courage and sensitivity.

Anger Without Action

We observed that David had lost his moral grip on the kingdom when he failed to respond properly to Amnon's sin against Tamar. Although he was furious with Amnon, he did nothing. Even though it was within his power and his office to bring Amnon to judgment and restore his daughter's self-respect, he did nothing. Having vented his righteous anger, he failed to act. Therefore David must bear the responsibility for creating a moral vacuum that led to Tamar's enduring despair and Absalom's vigilante justice.

Well-meaning morality that fails to move from emotion to practice is a sure sign of a worn-out morality. The consequence of moral inaction is complicity in immorality. However, before we harshly condemn David's failure, we ought to acknowledge our own. Like David we are guilty of being "furious" with some evils without the follow-through of moral action. We have acquiesced to the status quo. Beyond emotional rhetoric we have done little about broken marriages, teenage rebellion, middle-aged affluence, abortion, premarital sex, and the idolatry of sports. Blowing up at some of these evils is not the same as discerning just ways of constructively dealing with them.

Remorse Without Reconciliation

David also frustrated Absalom by his inability to initiate reconciliation. His heart longed for Absalom but he was unwilling to take the first step to bring about judgment and forgiveness. His weakness before the sin of Amnon led to a rigidity with Absalom. David felt conflicting emotions toward his third son. Absalom had deceived him and killed his eldest son; yet, he still loved him and desired his fellowship. Absalom's three-year exile in Geshur and two-year estrangement in Jerusalem were painful for father and son alike, but apparently David felt the necessity of a hard-line position.

In this case David is typical of the moralist who reacts to evil by simply removing the sinner from his presence. Given David's convenient, yet sad example, the best way to deal with the divorced, the addict, and the homosexual is to ostracize them. Make them feel they are out in the cold. Ignore them. Neglect them. Treat them like they have the plague. If the church cannot minister to those who have fallen, to whom can it minister? This does not mean that the church is to warmly receive unrepentant sinners and blindly overlook their evil. It means that the church must take the initiative in encouraging and helping people to repent of their evil and be reconciled to God and man.

When David finally received Absalom, it was too late. The habits of the heart were firmly entrenched in his son's life. It was Absalom, not David, who finally took the initiative. Absalom forced David to receive him. It was either acceptance or death, and Absalom risked his life, counting on David's moral failure of nerve. Nothing is said of Amnon or Tamar. Apparently the past is ignored. Repentance and forgiveness go unmentioned.

Authority Without Accountability

David's ethical insensitivity and moral laxity were also apparent in his failure to claim responsibility for what transpired in the kingdom. Absalom is allowed to mastermind a conspiracy. He was able to steal the hearts of the people of Israel because David afforded him the opportunity. It is difficult to imagine Absalom's public relations coup going unnoticed by the king and his officials. For four years Absalom was allowed to challenge David's leadership publicly. He used the people's legitimate justice concerns to promote himself. As the king, David could not responsibly say, "I'll mind my own business and leave Absalom alone." David was not at liberty to dismiss the question casually, "What harm can Absalom do to me?" David's position included a moral responsibility to guard his people from deception. His refusal to act against Absalom not only threatened himself but allowed the people to be led astray. If David had held his office with a proper sense of accountability, he would not have allowed Absalom the freedom to undermine the kingdom.

By virtue of being a parent, a teacher, a citizen, an employer, an accountant, a merchant, a nurse, we have a responsibility to pursue justice in our sphere of work. With authority comes accountability. We cannot be a parent and disclaim parental responsibility. If we work for a firm that is illegally dumping pollutants, we have a responsibility to report that activity. It is our business. If we serve as an elder in the church, the moral integrity of the church body is our responsibility.

We might wish to turn a blind eye to moral offenses but our responsibility cannot be escaped. We cannot behave like an ostrich and pretend the problems will go away. We indict ourselves when we claim, "I see no evil, I hear no evil, I know no evil!" From God's perspective we are our "brother's keeper." A moral claim embraces our lives personally, vocationally, socially, and politically.

David's Legacy

I believe that David remained a serious worshiper throughout his life. If his last words are any indication, his personal spirituality remained vital. But in the closing years of his reign he abdicated much of his moral responsibility. Weakened through his own sin, especially in the matter of Bathsheba and Uriah, he made some grave mistakes. He became reactive rather than proactive. He seemed surprised by the moral demands confronting his administration. Time and again he defaulted on his leadership responsibilities and let circumstances run their course.

David's moral weakness is a reminder to the North American church. Like David, we have the symptoms of a worn-out morality: anger without action, remorse without reconciliation, and positions of authority without moral accountability. Perhaps we are like the church at Laodicea described in the book of Revelation (3:15–16): "I know your deeds," says the Ruler of God's creation, "that you are neither cold nor hot. I wish you were either one or the other! So, because you are lukewarm—neither hot nor cold—I am about to spit you out of my mouth." We are rich in convenience and comfort, but poor when it comes to ethical sensitivity and moral action. On camera we are everyone's envy but morally we are in tatters. Popular forms of evangelism and worship preclude serious moral reflection and ethical response. There appears to be little patience to understand and live according to the ethic of Jesus. We seem eager to abandon thinking and let the culture dictate our "Christian" response.

The account of Absalom and the latter days of his father's reign comprise a sad chapter in David's long life.

We may be thankful that the story does not end with Absalom's folly.

QUESTIONS FOR DISCUSSION

1. Do you agree that your ethical perspectives have been shaped and influenced by your relational and cultural background?
2. Do you believe there is a difference between your inherited perception of worldliness and a more biblical understanding of worldliness?
3. Is the observance of a Sabbath rest necessarily legalistic?
4. How does a shallow understanding of the Christian life contribute to moral weakness and ethical immaturity?
5. Do you believe there is a reluctance on the part of the church to nurture Christians in what it means to follow the ethic of Jesus in every sphere of life?
6. What are the signs of a worn-out morality?
7. Do you agree that it may be very important for Christians to pray for a greater measure of moral energy and ethical sensitivity?
8. Do you agree that many people avoid serious ethical reflection because they equate morality with a moralistic and legalistic outlook?

5

The Roots of Wisdom

The fear of the Lord is the beginning of wisdom.
Proverbs 9:10

Solomon succeeded David on Israel's throne. Unlike Absalom he sought to build his life on the moral strength of his father. He walked "according to the statutes of his father David." Instead of reacting to David's moral feebleness, as Absalom did, he remembered his father's righteous and upright heart. He saw himself as the benefactor of God's great kindness to his father. He was a true son of David.

Three important factors contributed to Solomon's desire for a discerning heart: He acknowledged God's vocational call on his life; he understood God's commands and sought to obey them; and he accepted his moral responsibility as king.

An Understanding Heart

There was no question in Solomon's mind that he had not succeeded to his father's throne on his own strength and merit. He understood the call of God: "Now, O LORD my God, you have made your servant king in place of my father David" (1 Kings 3:7). Solomon's humble acceptance of the sovereignty of God was clearly different from Absalom's self-appointed quest for success.

Solomon does not fit the model of the self-made professional. He did not pride himself on his own achievement or independence. His threefold reference to being God's servant reveals his self-perception. He humbly acknowledged, "I am only a little child and do not know how to carry out my duties" (3:7). Solomon allowed himself the personal honesty to be vulnerable before God. He was unashamed to reveal his dependency on the living God.

Solomon understood both the call of God on his life and the commands of God for his life. He demonstrated his love for the Lord "by walking according to the statutes of his father David." Solomon internalized the ethic of David and obeyed from the heart the precepts of God's Law. Wisdom was definite and practical. He had learned "the central point of Israel's faith, which is the meeting of life-in-the-world with life-before-God."[1]

Solomon was streetwise. He knew how to live in the real world. There was only one kind of wisdom worth knowing—the kind that would get you through life in one piece. Solomon found that wisdom in the statutes of God. He did not find wisdom among an elite academy of sophisticated sages. Nor did he measure wisdom by taking an opinion poll. Solomon found his real-world wisdom where every other Israelite could find it, in the Law of God. There were many other places he could have looked for

[1]Oliver O'Donovan, *Resurrection and the Moral Order* (Grand Rapids: Eerdmans, 1986), p. 189.

wisdom, and eventually he did; but in the beginning the precepts of God guided his life. God's wisdom was equally applicable to king and peasant alike. It was an accessible wisdom, a people's wisdom, taught to young and old, rich and poor. The Hebrews talked about this wisdom at the breakfast table and in the fields. Real-world living meant living responsibly before the Author of life. There was no secret about where to find this wisdom.

Solomon's humility before God was a moral attribute reminiscent of his father David. He saw himself among the people of God, as a member-in-community. The wording of his prayer contradicts the individualism of our own era: "Your servant is here among the people you have chosen, a great people, too numerous to count or number" (1 Kings 3:8). Solomon takes his place among the people. He is there to fulfill God's vocational call upon his life. His goal was not career advancement but the welfare of the people of God. The reign of the imperial self must bow to the responsibility of the servant. For Solomon the role of king could not be defined by the surrounding kingdoms but by the Lord of Israel and his statutes. Solomon was to be a steward, a manager, an administrator of God's people. He did not confuse stewardship with ownership and usurp the authority of God.

Solomon was awed by his responsibilities. "Who is able to govern this great people of yours?" he asked (3:9). He felt the need for wisdom and understanding. He sought the moral energy that only God could give for the task before him. His heart was receptive. On the night Solomon envisioned this conversation with God, he demonstrated the true search for excellence. In that moment he was light-years away from Absalom's self-reliant, self-serving, self-styled quest for success. Solomon came as a servant, a humble child, impressed with his own inadequacy and the greatness of the task. He came willing to receive from God the wisdom required to fulfill the responsibilities entrusted to him.

A Receptive Heart

The first step in educating the heart is the fear of God. Unless we humbly acknowledge our need for God and obediently submit to God's commands we will be swept downstream by the habits of the heart. Solomon was blessed with a spiritual legacy that enabled him to open his heart to the wisdom of God. He might have chosen to react against his father's moral weakness the way Absalom did; instead, he chose to fear the Lord. We are confronted by a similar choice. We need to learn from our moral and spiritual legacy. We must reject what is bad and turn to what is good.

Why do some people with very immoral backgrounds, who have been victims of abuse, poverty, or overindulgence, have such receptive hearts toward God, while others, who experience every moral advantage—a loving family, a good church, a fine education—have no interest in cultivating a discerning heart? No matter what kind of morality or immorality a person has been exposed to, the decision for or against a moral character belongs to the individual. The person is not a mere product of his moral environment. Behavioral conditioning cannot explain away ethical accountability. It is by God's grace that some who suffer tremendous moral privation are challenged to seek what is good and repudiate evil. They have learned through their experience with evil to desire the good.

Moral adversity can clarify a person's spiritual condition by either strengthening his resolve to obey God or undermining his faithfulness. Absalom was unable to cope with the moral pain of his sister's rape. His bitter rage destroyed whatever moral education Absalom had acquired from his father David. We need to stop and assess our own moral condition. Are we harboring a bitterness or animosity in our heart that is destroying our character?

Instead of feeling self-righteous and superior when confronted by evil and victimized by injustice, we can be led to examine ourselves. A victim of Klaus Barbie's brutality in a Nazi concentration camp was asked at Barbie's trial how he felt when he saw Barbie in the courtroom. His eyes filled with tears and he said, "I see myself." He reasoned that if an average-looking man like Barbie could commit horrendous atrocities, he too was capable of such evil.

The Russian dissident Aleksandr Solzhenitsyn suffered greatly for his opposition against injustices perpetrated by the Communist government. But the evil inhumanity of his captors was not the only reality that impressed Solzhenitsyn in the Gulag:

> It was only when I lay there on rotting prison straw that I sensed within myself the first stirrings of good. Gradually, it was disclosed to me that the line separating good and evil passes, not through states, nor between classes, nor between political parties either, but right through every human heart, and through all human hearts. So, bless you, prison, for having been in my life.[2]

It is important for us to discern the roots of wisdom and foolishness in our lives and learn from our past. But we cannot use our moral heritage as an excuse for becoming hard-hearted, turning away from God, intent on doing our own thing. We need to be honest with ourselves and ask if we really want the consequences of Absalom's "success ethic."

Another difficult question is the part Christian conversion plays in ethical sensitivity and moral maturity. Why do some people, who have nothing to do with Jesus Christ, stand head and shoulders above many Christians in integrity, compassion, and concern for justice? Obviously the demonstration of moral character is not limited to Christians. We can be grateful for the fact that God's grace is shed abroad in the hearts of all humankind, whether

[2]Aleksandr I. Solzhenitsyn, *The Gulag Archipelago* , III–IV (New York: Harper & Row, 1975), pp. 615-16.

people acknowledge him or not. We are made in the image of God and still reflect God's character even though we are damaged by sin.

True moral sensitivity leads not only to acts of kindness but also to an awareness of sin. God's grace is therefore evident among unbelievers in their acts of goodness and in their understanding of evil, though they usually recognize the evil of others and the systemic evil of society more than their own evil ways.

There are many professing Christians, believers in name only, who have never experienced Christian conversion or taken the ethic of Jesus seriously. A true spiritual conversion involves a turning away from evil and a turning toward righteousness through the acceptance and forgiveness of Christ. A genuine transformation of the soul is a transformation of one's life. Conversion is a work of grace. We do not merit salvation by our good efforts. We freely receive God's provision of salvation through our personal commitment to Jesus Christ. However, God's grace is not cheap grace. To believe in Jesus is to obey Jesus. The Christian ought to be involved in a continual conversion that involves a deepening passion for Christ and moral maturity.

No Guarantees

A true moral legacy is no guarantee that a person will form Christian character and make wise ethical decisions. All the prayer in the world may not prevent a person from turning his back on God and the moral life. In the previous chapter we explored the possible impact of David's worn-out morality on his son Absalom, but this does not remove Absalom's responsibility to act in accord with the truth he knows. Solomon benefited from his father's example, Absalom chose not to.

The following account may sound hackneyed, because it reminds you of an unimaginative television plot. I can assure you it does not sound the least bit hackneyed to those who care for the family involved. Patty grew up in a thoughtful Christian home, married a Christian she had known for years, and seemingly had everything a young woman could want. She and Bill had two healthy, beautiful daughters and a lot of encouragement from both sides of an extended Christian family. They were active in a couple's Bible study, and Bill was a lay leader in their church. They had what a lot of people dream of having: economic security, happy children, and an encouraging, caring, extended family.

Their life was comfortable and convenient, but for Patty it seemed dull and unromantic. Then she met a man who managed a local drugstore. It started innocently enough. He flirted with her whenever she came into the store. She loved the attention. Just the fact that another man was noticing her sparked a sense of excitement. They began seeing each other. As she tells it in stock phrases that sound canned, Dan made her feel important, overcame her boredom, and rekindled her romantic passion. She started skipping the women's Bible study she was in. She would leave the kids with her husband and rendezvous with Dan; even the deception seemed exciting. She was actually playing the leading role in a plot she had watched repeatedly on TV. But this time she was part of the drama.

When Bill eventually found out, he went out and had his own affair, just to prove that two can play the same game. Both lashed out at each other. They blamed each other. Patty claimed that she fell for Dan because Bill never paid any attention to her. He was too wrapped up in his work to give her the love she needed and deserved. Even their excuses and accusations sounded like a cheap TV script.

They played it cool for a while. They showed up at Bible studies as if nothing was wrong and kept up with church activities. Patty kept seeing Dan. It was inevitable, though, in a small town, that the news would eventually get out. Patty's parents were devastated. They would have found a violent mugging less painful. Their hearts ached for Patty, for Bill, for their granddaughters, for themselves. They wept. "Where did we go wrong?" they asked. "Could we have done something to prevent it?" In fact, Patty blamed them and falsely accused them, "You forced me to marry Bill. I never loved him. I only married him to please you." She resented everyone but Dan. No guilt. No remorse. "It was time," she said, "to do something for myself."

It is difficult to account for Patty's immoral decisions. She had all the advantages of growing up in a loving home. Patty was taught the difference between right and wrong, but, more importantly, she experienced the security and joy found in a home where mother and father loved one another and honored Christ. Moral-order parenting was no guarantee that Patty would remain faithful to Christ and benefit from the example offered to her.

The moralist reads Proverbs 22:6 as a guarantee: "Train a child in the way he should go, and when he is old he will not turn from it." However, Solomon intended it to be an encouragement, not a guarantee. He was making an observation not a prediction. Moralistic thinking defines "train a child in the way he should go" in terms of religious requirements. The child must be indoctrinated in the "things of God." This can include faithful church attendance, Christian school education or perhaps home-school education, and separation from the world as much as possible. "Train a child" means telling the child what to do and what not to do. It means giving the child answers and telling the child how to think. Moralists want to follow a recipe. If they stir in all the right ingredients and bake it at the right temperature, the finished product is guaranteed. Without a firm foothold in character, the moralist slides between leniency and legalism.

Moral-Order Parenting

Character development does not work that way. Character is not assembled, it is nurtured. Christians with an educated heart do not fall off an assembly line. We can't take out a manual and assemble a child into a justice-seeking Christian who is thoughtful, compassionate, and faithful.

Moral-order thinking approaches parenting different-ly. Training a child does not consist of a set of requirements or a list of dos and don'ts. Obedience and self-discipline are taught by example and instruction not indoctrination. They are modeled by the behavior and character of the parent. The child is taught how to think, not simply what to think. Parent and child interact in a way that reinforces question-ing and dialogue. Moral-order parenting disciplines and punishes, but does not reject, as David did with Absalom. Obedience to the statutes of God is not a matter of compliance but a matter of the heart.

Training a child in the way he should go involves teaching children how to make moral decisions. And the best way for parents to do that is to live each day consciously aware of the moral impact of their lives. Moralists put children into schools, programs, and safe environments. Moral-order parents exemplify for their children how to live in a broken, hurting world. And they hold their children accountable to their example.

There are many reasons why some learn languages better than others, but I find the difference between moralistic parenting and moral-order parenting analogous to different methods of learning a foreign language. I struggled through language classes always hoping that the teacher would not call on me. I spent hours trying to memorize my vocabulary and declensions—not because I wanted to learn the language, but because I didn't want to be embarrassed when the teacher called on me. The all-important objective was to pass the tests with a respectable grade. I hated the nervous, uncomfortable feeling of struggling with a foreign language. Like the moralistic parent, my teacher expected a performance. I could avoid poor grades and embarrassment by complying with her expectations. But I learned very little. The language never became a part of me.

It was a different story for my wife, who spent fifteen years in Brazil. Ginny grew up overhearing Portuguese and quickly learned to interact with her Brazilian friends. She didn't learn the language so she could pass a test. There was no separation between the classroom and the rest of her life when it came to learning Portuguese. She was only half conscious of the learning process. When she was surrounded by Brazilians at school, at play, at the market, or at church, she spoke and thought in Portuguese. When she wanted to say something she didn't have to translate mentally from English to Portuguese. The Portuguese came out as easily as English. I tried to learn a language so I could fulfill school requirements. Ginny learned Portuguese so she could interact with Brazilians. In moral-order parenting the language of Christian faith and action is learned by involvement, interaction, and internalization. It becomes the grammar of daily life and the vocabulary of shared convictions.

Focus on the Generations

Moral-order parenting has a long history. When Moses gave God's commands to the people of Israel, he also gave them an instructional method. He taught them how to teach their children. At the core of Moses' pedagogical approach was a profound personal love for God. "Love the LORD your God with all your heart and with all your soul and with all your strength" (Deut. 6:5). Parents could not begin to be successful with their children's moral instruction if they lacked this essential relational commitment.

The parent's second responsibility was to appreciate the social impact of their personal faith. Obedience was an investment in future generations. Observe God's commandments, Moses told the people, so that "you, your children and their children after them may fear the LORD your God as long as you live by keeping all his decrees and commands that I give you, and so that you may enjoy long life" (Deut. 6:2). Any privatized, individualized notion of one's faith was to be dispelled by the deeply felt awareness that personal obedience had a direct bearing on future generations. Furthermore, the joy of living resulted from an obedient consideration of the welfare of others. To live only for oneself was to work against one's self.

The third responsibility assured the relevancy of the commandments to daily living. Parents were instructed to internalize the statutes of God. "These commandments," Moses emphasized, "are to be upon your hearts." Obedience was not a matter of compliance with a list of prohibitions. It was not an external code that people tolerated. Righteousness involved a heartfelt conviction about how to live life significantly. A doctor can put a cardiac patient on a diet, but if the patient sees no relationship between diet and health or complies with the diet simply to please the doctor, the chances of the patient's staying on the diet are greatly reduced. The patient has to own the responsibility for eating right for his or her own sake. Taking the commandments of God to heart required believing in the practical, life-related value of God's will for everyday living.

The fourth responsibility dealt with the actual method of instructing children in the commandments of God. "Impress them on your children," urged Moses. "Talk about them when you sit at home and when you walk along the road, when you lie down and when you get up" (Deut. 6:7). There was to be no division between the classroom and real world. Theory and practice were combined. The parental commentary was to be a dialogue, not a monologue. The whole learning process depended upon meaningful interaction between parent and child. Questions were encouraged and no "because I said so" answers were allowed. Moses gave very specific instruction on this point; "When your son asks you, "What is the meaning of the stipulations, decrees and laws the LORD our

God has commanded you?" tell him how God powerfully rescued us from slavery in Egypt and gave us his commands "so that we might always prosper and be kept alive" (6:20, 24). The pedagogical principles given by God and introduced by Moses still apply today. They make the difference between a lasting moral legacy or moral bankruptcy. The goal of moral-order parenting has always been heart righteousness and character formation.

David's legacy was by no means a perfect example of moral-order parenting. David failed Absalom and Tamar when he chose to ignore Amnon's sin and allow Tamar's disgrace to remain. In many ways David's relationship with Absalom seems out-of-character. His heart for righteousness was hardened by anger without action, remorse without reconciliation, and royal authority without moral accountability. But the strength of his moral character came through for Solomon. His love for God and a passion for righteousness profoundly influenced his son and led to Solomon's life-changing request for a discerning heart. Solomon was able to discern the central point of his father's life, which was the meeting of life-in-the-world with life-before-God.[3] Solomon's honest, humble fear of God overruled the habits of the heart and inspired him to seek a discerning heart, which is an educated heart.

QUESTIONS FOR DISCUSSION

1. In what sense is Solomon the antithesis of Absalom?
2. Do you believe that Solomon's advancement is an appropriate model for success in the business world or in the academic community?
3. Do you agree that moral maturity depends more on humble submission to the revealed will of God than it does on human ingenuity?

[3]Oliver O'Donovan, *Resurrection and the Moral Order* (Grand Rapids: Eerdmans, 1986), p.187.

4. To what degree is a person a product of his moral environment?
5. Why is Christian conversion so essential to Christian morality?
6. Do you agree that moral-order parenting does not guarantee that children will automatically follow the moral wisdom of their parents?
7. Do you think our sense of moral responsibility would be greater if we were more concerned about the moral character of our children and our children's children?
8. What are some of the practical steps that should be taken to help the next generation toward ethical maturity?

6

A Discerning Heart

If any of you lacks wisdom, he should ask God . . .
                                                James 1:5

The business of giving advice to the American people
is a 15-billion-dollar-a-year growth industry. In vast numbers people are turning to strangers, specialists in the
behavioral sciences, who are trained to hear their most
personal problems at an hourly rate. These properly
certified experts are emotional accountants who help figure
out our psychological credits and debits. Like master
mechanics tuning a complex precision-built engine, they
help regulate the intricate, modern psyche. They adjust our
emotional carburetor, change our conceptual filters, slow
down our idle speed so we can hear ourselves think. It is
difficult to imagine how we could protect ourselves from
the onslaughts of the sexual revolution, family breakdown,
and our pervasive feeling of malaise without calling into
active duty an army of therapists, counselors, psychologists,
and consultants.

Independently minded Americans have never required more assistance than they do today. Ironically, the American quest for autonomy has as its by-product a growing dependency on a vast assortment of therapies. This search for self-sovereignty has also contributed to drug and alcohol dependency. As the influence of the extended family and the church decreases, the need for "professional" counsel increases. Therapy has become a major component of the burgeoning service industry. In a consumer society we grow accustomed to paying for services we used to do for ourselves. Twenty years ago a major franchise such as Quik Lube, designed with the single purpose of giving your car an oil change in ten minutes, was unheard of. There is nothing wrong with having your car's oil changed in ten minutes. I think it's a great idea. I am concerned, however, that the same kind of mentality might influence how we approach the moral life.

Making it in the real world today too often means knowing where to go to have your feelings serviced and your perspective fixed. We seek out an expert, usually a stranger, to discover ourselves. The specialist views our "problem" from an approach to life that is expected to have no moral bearing on his advice. The therapist's morality is never debated. The psychologist's worldview is never discussed. The counselor's character and family life are considered immaterial to the client's particular need. The "professional" maintains his or her personal distance. Involvement is safely limited to a scheduled appointment. The overall effect of this mentality does not make the American more independent and self-assured. The opposite is true. People become dependent on the impersonal influence of arbitrary information selected from an uncontested worldview. The client lets the therapists mold his thinking without any claim to moral authority. The "full-service" marketplace mentality means that everything is done for us, even our thinking, for a fee.

Interior Decorators

People are doing with their lives what they do with their living rooms. In upscale middle-class homes the living room exists for show, and the family room for television. The rest of the house may have that lived-in look, but the living room is reserved for formal occasions. The decorum of the living room is too important to be left to chance. It is a fashion statement. If you are really serious about interior decorating, you don't go to the furniture store and pick out a few pieces and then drop in at the paint store for wallpaper and at Sears for drapes. You need professional advice. You need the assurance that what you are putting together will impress your guests and make the right statement about who you are. Home decorating is not an easy task given the vast array of styles, fabrics, colors and designs, but with the expert advice of a professional interior designer, you can create a picture-perfect room.

There are similarities between creating a fashionable living room and organizing our lives. A customized lifestyle and a showpiece living room may have more in common than we think. Both how we design our lives and how we arrange our living rooms ultimately become arbitrary, merely a matter of preference and taste. The standard changes according to what is "in" or "out" of home decorating fashion.

Without the conviction of an authoritative moral order, the decision for or against casual sex or a homosexual lifestyle is ultimately arbitrary, even though potentially traumatic. The search for our "true" selves is made much more difficult by no other "moral" standard than the habits of the heart. Success and self-fulfillment are determined more by peer pressure than God-given principle. Generally speaking, the advice industry has become fashionable rather than faithful. Wisdom from God has been forgotten and in some cases despised in exchange for a relativized array of "moral" options. Who is to say what is right or wrong when moral values are self-determined and social acceptance is based on public relations? Publicity not principle decides the moral outlook of modern man and woman in the heartland of America. Madison Avenue and Hollywood are to American morality what *Better Homes and Gardens* is to home decorating. The remodeling of morality is advertised for popular consumption. We want to become what we see.

A curious feature of home decorating magazines is the absence of people in their pictures of beautifully decorated rooms. There is no sign of life in the living room. The room is designed for show not for living. Real people are as out of place there as they are in approaches to ethics that reduce the moral life to "interior decorating." Rearranging perspectives will not take away guilt any more than rearranging the furniture in your living room will. Morality does not follow fashion. It is not trendy and arbitrary. The moral life does not consist of decorating one's perspectives in the latest lifestyles. It consists of a deep human desire for a discerning heart that recognizes the moral standard, not of our own making, but of God's revealing.

A Request

Solomon built upon David's spiritual legacy by making a simple request. He asked God for a "discerning heart" to govern God's people and "to distinguish between right and wrong." He was convinced of God's moral authority and was sensitive to his role as servant. Solomon was conscious of his moral need and aware of how difficult it was to distinguish between right and wrong. Therefore he asked for the ability to administer justice out of a heart perceptively aware of God's will. Ethics must be shaped by the earnest request for God's counsel. Moral-order thinking begins with this profound, simple desire to be in harmony with the mind of God, to be a person after God's own heart.

You can tell a great deal about a person from what he or she asks for. Our requests reveal who we are. Solomon's prayer for a receptive heart showed that he was ready to receive and submit to God's perspective. God does not force morality upon us. Unless we are willing recipients of God's wisdom, we will not be beneficiaries of his wisdom. We are held accountable for this desire, just as Solomon was, but even the desire in our heart is an expression of God's grace toward us.

God acknowledged that there were many things Solomon might have requested, such as health, wealth, and the destruction of his enemies, but God commended Solomon for choosing the one thing most needful—a wise and discerning heart (1 Kings 3:11). We are told that the Lord was "pleased" with Solomon's request. It would be easy for us to pass over this observation and not recognize its importance. Perhaps we are unaccustomed to acknowledging God's emotional response to our requests. The Lord finds pleasure in Solomon's desire for a discerning heart. Like a parent pleased with the personal choices of his child, God finds satisfaction in our humble request for wisdom.

Parents usually learn the hard way not to give certain things to their child until the child really wants them. Great gifts given before a child can appreciate them end up either broken or ignored. The joy of giving and receiving depends on the child's development. The child must be ready to receive what the parent has desired all along to give. Solomon showed that he was ready to receive moral guidance from God. What God thought of him and what God had to give him meant more to Solomon than health or wealth.

There are many deceptions and sinful complexities that dissuade us from making this simple, obvious request from God. Since the strategies of self-deception are many and the confusion surrounding life priorities is great, we cannot take Solomon's request for granted. His simple, straightforward appeal to God may be the hardest thing for us to do. The profound simplicity of Solomon's request for a discerning heart may appear unrealistic in light of the world's complexities. It sounds too simple. How can moral-order thinking begin with such an unpretentious premise—namely, that the fear of God is the beginning of wisdom? Is this where we begin when we deal with nuclear weapons, surrogate motherhood, greed, sexual ethics, and a host of other equally challenging issues? How can we expect the lawyer, the scientist, and the politician to begin here, with a sincere desire for a discerning heart?

To those trained in the technicalities of the law and the complexities of technology and politics, this request may sound idealistic, platitudinous, and anachronistic. What does a personal conversation with God have to do with making it in the real world of "lasers in the jungle"? It makes all the difference in the world. The key to moral wisdom and ethical insight is not to be found in volumes of philosophical debate covering every moral contingency, but in a profound relational commitment to the Author of life.

Let me try to illustrate what I mean. When Ginny and I decided it was time to draw up a will, we went to a lawyer. We wanted a simple will declaring that when one of us dies the other is the beneficiary. And when we both die our property is to be divided equally among our three children. Nothing complicated, right? No. The lawyer drew up twelve pages of legal wording in fine print covering every kind of contingency. The legal language was so technical I had to keep asking him for a translation. Our lawyer was doing his job and in the process proved the point that nothing is simple in law, especially for the layman. That legal document is now filed away along with old tax returns and appliance warranties. It has absolutely no effect on my daily life. It is there if a lawyer needs to prove what should take place normally at our deaths.

Now it was a different story when Ginny and I were married. We did not sign a contract, we made a commitment. Before God and in the presence of family and friends we exchanged vows. We did not debate the intricacies of a legal contract covering all the possible contingencies that could affect our marriage though ultimately such contingencies are far more complex and challenging than any that might affect disposal of wealth. We committed ourselves to each other in unguarded, unqualified, comprehensive language. The vows I made on that day affect every day of my life. Those few simple words expressed once and for all the desire of my heart to be committed to one and only one woman forever. I can renew my vows, but I cannot add to their lasting effect.

Solomon's request for a discerning heart is much more like a simple marriage vow than a complex contract. The request reveals the desire of his heart. Through it we understand his commitment to the Lord. His prayer underscores his solemn and significant personal, inner-man, disposition to God's moral order. Solomon's request does not draw attention to his cleverness and ingenuity but to his personal commitment to the authority of God's moral perspective. Out of this conviction he is able to cultivate the ability to see all the angles of a particular moral problem. The reflective, intellectual ability follows from a passionate, single-minded desire for God's wisdom.

Therefore it is important for us to emphasize the profound simplicity of a discerning heart that seeks God's wisdom. The well-known, one-line ethical imperatives of the Bible underscore the spiritual dimension that is absolutely crucial to moral-order thinking. All the moral debates in the world mean nothing apart from the foundational command to "love the LORD your God with all your heart and with all your soul and with all your strength" (Deut. 6:5). What is the use of searching out all the positions and complexities of a moral issue if we refuse to hear the voice of the prophet saying, "He has showed you, O man what is good. And what does the LORD require of you? To act justly and to love mercy and to walk humbly with your God" (Micah 6:8).

Ethics and spirituality cannot be compartmentalized. They rest on one single desire, which was clearly expressed by Jesus when he commanded, "Seek first his kingdom and his righteousness" (Matt. 6:33). This statement is not a simplistic reduction of the Christian faith to a tenet of traditional religion; rather, it is an all-embracing, personal comprehension of the whole counsel of God. Such commitment moves us in the strong current of God's will.

When Paul said to the Corinthians, "For I resolved to know nothing while I was with you except Jesus Christ and him crucified" (1 Cor. 2:2), he was not disqualifying the hard work of ethical reflection and moral action. He was not implying that the church should be uninvolved in social justice or medical ethical issues. Sincere but misguided Christians cannot use this verse to distance the church from the problems of abortion, affluence, and apartheid. If we are to be consistent with the example of the apostle Paul, we will take the ethic of the Cross and apply it to every sphere of life just the way Paul did for the Corinthians.

The intent reflected in these biblical "one-liners" is not reductionistic but comprehensive. On the one hand, they expose the foolishness of celebrated one-liners fashionable in pop morality such as "If it feels good, do it" or "I'm OK; you're OK"; on the other, they express the wisdom of the true art of living. Solomon's simple request sets the tone for moral decision making. It is not a frantic search for the right answer amidst a confusing array of complex alternatives. It is a profound, heartfelt turning to God and discovering the enduring relevancy and permanent applicability of God's wisdom.

Wisdom's Rainbow

The book of Proverbs describes the rich beauty and sheer brilliance of God's wisdom. It is as if the pure light of God's wisdom struck the prism of life and flashed colorful rays in every direction, each ray reflecting the character of wisdom and the appealing glow of the educated heart. The resulting rainbow of constituent colors represents the multi-faceted nature of true wisdom.[1]

The first chapter of Proverbs offers a word picture of wisdom's rainbow. As you stop and read the first chapter of Proverbs, I think you will agree with me. The skilled artist sketches in simple beauty the deep aspirations of the soul, found not in lavish rhetoric and flowery language, but in the familiar words descriptive of what is irreplaceable for practical living. The moral landscape is best described with words such as insight, discernment, discretion, guidance, common sense, and understanding. Character is colored in the earth tones of life-related wisdom necessary for daily living. Without this insight, living becomes a lost art, displaced by worthless imitations without moral value.

The solar energy of the moral universe is the fear of the Lord. The most advanced technology of our day, in and of itself, will not enable us to access the wisdom of God. What was true in Job's day is still true in ours. State-of-the-art technology, divorced from the fear of the Lord, offers no hope (Job 28). If the wonders of creation and the cultivating ingenuity of man are cut off from the Creator, even the most marvelous scientific discoveries will not lead us to Wisdom. Discernment is not to be found on the frontiers of the biomedical revolution or in the technological breakthroughs of the twenty-first century. Only God knows the way to understanding. Material success and cultural sophistication are of no advantage in obtaining true wisdom and very well may prove to be great hindrances. Apart from an openhearted receptivity to all that God has to offer, we will not see the clear light of wisdom's rainbow. It is only as we fear the Lord and shun evil that we begin the process of educating the heart in a life of wisdom.

We should also add that the fear of the Lord does not depreciate common sense and the intellect. Too many Christians divorce the two and disparage our God-given

[1]Derek Kidner, *Proverbs* (Downers Grove, Ill.: InterVarsity, 1964), p. 36.

capacity to think and reason. The anti-intellectualism of
many Christians flies in the face of the biblical model
presented in Proverbs, which integrates spirituality, sensible cultural custom, and practical common sense. Recently
someone wrote to me suggesting that I "renounce all
knowledge which is not *necessary* for mankind." Of course,
he felt he knew from his vantage point what was unnecessary and, although he did not spell it out, he would
probably eliminate in one sweep history, literature, philosophy, sociology, anthropology, and political science from
the Christian's curriculum. He emphasized that "behind all
of this knowledge stands the devil to distract man from the
Truth." It is sad, but some Christians use their piety to
defend their lack of education. They may be very sincere,
but they have failed to apply the Word of God to life and to
take seriously the challenge to "take captive every thought
to make it obedient to Christ" (2 Cor. 10:5). We certainly
will not be able to "demolish arguments and every
pretension that sets itself up against the knowledge of God"
if we ignore the world around us and run from the
university. The educated heart cannot separate knowledge
from the fear of the Lord; neither does it seek to use the
fear of the Lord against knowledge. If we serve Christ, "in
whom are hidden all the treasures of wisdom and knowledge" we will honor and rejoice in the truth and will not be
deceived "by fine-sounding arguments," even arguments
that disparage knowledge (Col. 2:3–4).

Moral-order living places life in orbit around a quality
of character reflecting spiritual devotion, moral perceptive-
ness, ethical discernment, self-discipline, and a teachable
spirit. Such wisdom is a far cry from the "dos-and-don'ts"
teachings of mindless moralism and the "if it feels good, do
it" attitude of relativism. Instruction is not made up of pat
answers, nor does moral training consist of a checklist of
prohibitions. The pursuit of wisdom is not the casual
pastime hobby of people who can afford optional luxuries.
It ought to be the basic quest of the human soul. Yet it is
the sad, sinful tendency of human nature to place life in

orbit around self, even though the wisdom necessary for living is unattainable if left to the habits of the heart.

A Life Picture

The book of Proverbs begins with a word picture of descriptive concepts used to delineate the many facets of wisdom and ends with a life picture portraying the quality of wisdom in the woman of noble character (Prov. 31). If our heartfelt desire for God's wisdom defines us, this character is displayed in our life patterns. The fruit of a discerning heart is expressed in the decisions, priorities, and activities of daily life.

There are many ways the book of Proverbs might have been concluded. Consider how a college professor might conclude a lecture series on wisdom—a unique subject indeed, considering current lecture topics. The professor's goal would probably be a concisely worded summary of the key principles of wisdom. As he or she offered carefully worded axioms, delineated with appropriate subpoints, students would try to write down word for word the theoretical description of wisdom, thinking as they write how they will memorize the material for the final exam.

Perhaps the final chapter of Proverbs might have been offered by an oriental sage, one who sat aloof from the business and busyness of life. Reflecting on the wisdom of his many years, he would commend the advantages of a quiet demeanor and a life of contemplation. He would extol the beauty of nature and offer a recital of common-sense sayings.

The most likely idea for a conclusion would probably be a description of wisdom in the life of the king. Perhaps a self-portrait by Solomon would best illustrate the character of wisdom. If this idea did occur to the writer, it may have been dismissed because so few of us can identify with the life of a king. The practical purpose of the book of Proverbs is that we understand and apply wisdom in the real world of family and work.

Instead of concluding with a carefully worded lecture on wisdom or the findings of a Confucius-like sage or the exemplary life of the king, the book closes with a portrait of a wise woman.

A moralistic approach to this final chapter in Proverbs makes it good sermon material for Mother's Day. The practical life-related wisdom of Proverbs suddenly is turned into an idealistic, almost mythical, ode to "super mom." I am confident that this is not what the writer intended. It was meant to be read as a life portrait of a person who feared the Lord and whose life pattern displayed this character. It is a realistic description of applied wisdom. The character of this noble woman shines through all the activities of her busy life. The quality of her character cannot be measured by an itemized list of activities nor is the beauty of her character judged by cosmetic charm. She is wise in the depth of her being because she fears the Lord. She surpasses women who do "noble things" and her beauty does not fade with age. Those closest to her see in her an example of God's grace and strength. Her family benefits from her confidence, discernment, and diligence. She has exchanged the flattery of superficial compliments for the praise of her character. This woman desires and demonstrates a discerning heart in everything she does.

The woman described in Proverbs 31 illustrates moral-order living. Her life exemplifies the multifaceted nature of true wisdom; it touches every area of life. She can work with her hands as well as with her mind. She is active in the home and outside the home. She cares for her family materially and spiritually. Yet she does not live entirely for her family. She gives herself to the poor and needy as well. There is a consistency and a coherence to her lifestyle. She is balanced but not bored, active but not hassled. She lives without excuses. Her spirituality is woven into the fabric of her life. She refuses to compartmentalize her activity into spiritual and secular categories. Her Mondays are as holy as her Sabbaths.

All that we see in this woman of noble character presents a beautiful portrait of wisdom's harmony. She is fulfilled within herself but not by herself. She is one with her husband and supportive of her children. Her life in all its dimensions is its own reward! She is worthy of praise. But her real reward is in her work, in her relationships, in the experience of God's wisdom in her life. She does not do things to get them over with so she can get on with her own life. Her fear of the Lord and humble service to the poor save her from self-righteousness.

Here is a woman who should be the practical model for every man and woman, but our culture is uncomfortable with the human greatness she typifies. Such greatness is of God and is expressed in justice, fidelity, and love. Moral-order living strikes this culture as uneventful and boring, because our fascination is with celebrities who are packaged for our consumption by the media. Notoriety is better than no recognition at all. The name of the game is being able to walk down the street and be noticed. Character has been discarded for style, perhaps because it is so much easier to imitate fashion than to exhibit a fear of God. It is not surprising that a culture that prides itself on everyone doing as they please should prefer to minimize qualities that truly set people apart. Apparently in today's media-conditioned imagination it is easier to think that what separates us from popular recognition is nothing other than big biceps, big bucks and sex appeal. We cast off the priceless portrait of wisdom for this month's centerfold and celebrity status. We exchange the image of God for the consuming image of popular attention.

The failure to respond positively to this life portrait of wisdom is not only a general problem in the culture but a specific problem among professing Christians. The testimony of many church attenders lacks the consistency and coherence of the life pattern exemplified in the character of this woman.

Popular perspectives among Christians on marriage help to illustrate the confusion and disorientation about life widespread among believers. Take Bill, for instance. On a Monday afternoon I received a phone call from him asking to see me right away. "It's not an emergency, but it is urgent," he said. Fifteen minutes later he was in my office, trying to catch his breath before telling me what was on his mind. I had seen Bill occasionally at church. He usually came late and left as soon as the worship service concluded. We had talked one other time over lunch, mainly about his divorce and his displeasure with one of the other businessmen in our church.

Still a bit winded, he forced out what he came for. "I want you to marry us," he said, rolling his eyes and shifting his weight. "Betty and I have decided to get married." "Who is Betty?" I asked. 'She's a believer who goes to a church about twenty miles from here." He paused. "But I don't remember the name of the church. We were going to get married in May, but we decided why put it off. We're ready."

'Well Bill," I began, "I would like to meet Betty and begin to see you both for counseling. We need to talk through your previous marriage." Bill looked uncomfortable and impatient and said, "We are thinking about a wedding this Friday. Betty's daughter can be here and my son can make it and we've thought a lot about this . . . and we want it Friday."

Bill was a sporadic church attender who had kept his distance from others in the church. I had never met Betty at church, and I found this unusual if their relationship had become that serious. Nor was I very confident Bill saw any value in spiritual direction. When he said they were getting married Friday(!) and this was Monday afternoon, I was dismayed. "Bill, I can't be involved if it's this Friday. Marriage is too important and too permanent to rush into. You have your previous marriage to work through. Spiritual direction before you make this commitment is essential." His lips tightened, his eyes rolled and he shifted his weight. "I have been an active member at this church for ten years. I'm a grown adult and it's not as if Betty and I haven't talked this over . . . a lot!"

Bill wanted me to perform a ceremony—a simple matter of giving up an hour or so of my time on Friday afternoon. No big deal, he thought; it can be easily scheduled. What right did I have meddling in their decisions. They wanted to get married and it was my job as a minister to do it. All he wanted from me was a "meaningful" ceremony. But I felt the responsibility to give them something they did not want, to deal with marriage as a life-commitment.

The fact that both Bill and Betty professed to be believers gave me no assurance that they understood God's wisdom on marriage or that their lives reflected the spiritual maturity and moral coherence practicing believers should demonstrate. It was not that they had to prove themselves so much as prepare themselves for the life they ought to live. Failure to distinguish between performing a wedding ceremony and serious preparation for marriage is as inexcusable as it is common. We have so much to say about the value of marriage but so little spiritual direction to offer to the couple. Little forethought is given to the "tools" of marriage: forgiveness, communication, worship, and the shared work of life together. Bill was in no mood for a delay. He knew what he wanted and when I didn't go along with him he was ready to look for another pastor. As he left my study he curtly informed me that I wouldn't see him at our church ever again. Bill wanted me to perform a wedding ceremony. I wanted to help him prepare for marriage.

There is a great contrast between the portrait of the wise woman and Bill's life. Their approaches to life are very different. Bill is trying to fit all the pieces of life together. He wants to give some role to the religious sphere of life; yet he wants to do his own thing, too. At the core of his being is a collage of hopes and desires. The fear of the Lord is not his central focus but he cannot admit that. The desire for a discerning heart is missing because he is too busy taking life one day at a time.

Christ Our Wisdom

Placed in the context of the book of Proverbs, Solomon's simple request for a discerning heart embraces the comprehensive scope of wisdom. Wisdom's word picture (chap. 1) and life portrait (chap. 31) describe the meaning of moral-order living. The fear of the Lord is a quality of being and a way of life. Ethics is founded on a personal relationship with the Author of wisdom. Therefore wisdom is not an abstract commodity, a listing of principles or a regimen of behavioral regulations. Wisdom is personal. It is the way of life that grows and develops from a living, vital relationship with the Creator of the universe.

In the eighth chapter of Proverbs wisdom is personified: "I, wisdom, dwell together with prudence; I possess knowledge and discretion. . . . I hate pride and arrogance, evil behavior and perverse speech. Counsel and sound judgment are mine; I have understanding and power" (8:12–14). This literary device underscores the personal quality of wisdom, but in addition to that, the personification unites the wisdom needed to live in the world (vv. 1–21) with the wisdom by which the world exists (vv. 22–31).[2] Therefore how we ought to live is guided by the same wisdom responsible for the very existence of life. Moral-order thinking is consistent with the created order. All that God creates bears the mark of his wisdom. Wisdom, embodied by God, precedes everything: "The LORD brought me forth as the first of his works, before his deeds of old; I was appointed from eternity, from the beginning, before the world began" (vv. 22–23). If we do not desire this wisdom, we do not desire what God himself uses to create. We do not desire life.

[2]Ibid., p. 79.

The early Christians read Proverbs 8 with Christ in mind. The fear of the Lord was defined for them more clearly than theretofore possible. God's wisdom became manifest through the incarnation of the eternal Son of God. The interface between the wisdom by which the world exists and the wisdom needed to live in the world was found in Jesus. The wisdom of creation and the moral order depended upon Jesus, their common personal source, who came to rescue us from evil.

> Through him all things were made; without him
> nothing was made that has been made. In him was
> life, and that life was the light of men. (John 1:3–4)

The meaning of the universe and of human behavior finds its ultimate explanation and validation in Jesus Christ, "in whom are hidden all the treasures of wisdom and knowledge" (Col. 2:3). In Jesus, we witness one greater than Solomon, who demonstrated through his life the desire for a discerning heart and through his teaching explained the comprehensive scope of God's kingdom ethic. Even more importantly he offered us this life-related wisdom through a personal relationship with himself. The process of educating the heart begins with our openness to all that God has promised to give us through Jesus Christ. The fear of the Lord is foundational to a discerning heart and is expressed in a life ethic rooted in a personal commitment to Jesus Christ who has become for us wisdom.

Solomon's request for wisdom and his understanding of wisdom's multifaceted nature and life pattern are even more relevant after the coming of Christ than they were before. Not only has the model been better illustrated in Jesus than in Solomon, but also the means to fulfill God's life ethic have passed from promise to accomplishment. The spiritual legacy left to us through Christ's teaching and life captures the essence of wisdom's word picture and life portrait. As we will see, the conventional wisdom of the world cannot be compared to the wisdom of the Cross.

God's unique gift of wisdom, illustrated in Solomon's test case, foreshadows the ethic of the Cross.

QUESTIONS FOR DISCUSSION

1. Who do people turn to when they become confused and discouraged with their lives?
2. How is interior decorating analogous to the way many people approach the matter of organizing their moral and spiritual life?
3. Does Solomon's request for a discerning heart parallel your own desire for wisdom?
4. Do you agree that a covenantal commitment to God is stronger and more comprehensive than a contractual agreement with God could ever be?
5. How are the qualities of wisdom noted in Proverbs a far cry from the "dos-and-don'ts" of a moralistic outlook and the "if it feels good, do it" attitude of relativism?
6. How does the life pattern of the woman of noble character reveal the wisdom of God?
7. Do you believe that Jesus embodied the wisdom we need today to live in the modern world? How does the ancient wisdom of the Word of God prepare us for living in the twenty-first century?

7

Solomon's Test Case

> *Away with the noise of your songs! I will not listen to the music of your harps. But let justice roll on like a river, righteousness like a never-failing stream!*
>
> Amos 5:23–24

When Solomon awoke, he realized he had been in a dream. His dialogue with God had taken place in his sleep. He had gone to Gibeon to participate in a highly publicized religious ceremony sponsored by the city's inhabitants. Like his father, Solomon sought to appease these original inhabitants of Canaan who lived only six miles from Jerusalem. Fostering good public relations with the Gibeonites was part of his job.

Solomon lived in a pluralistic culture. Not everyone shared the same worldview and life commitments. Solomon found it easier to placate divergent views on God and man than to confront them. We are told that he loved the Lord "by walking according to the statutes of his father

David, except that he offered sacrifices and burned incense on the high places" (1 Kings 3:3). This exception was a major weakness in Solomon's administration that eventually led to increased spiritual conflict in Solomon's life and work. Solomon's compromise with Gibeon was dictated by the conventional wisdom of his time and profession. When he offered a thousand burnt offerings on the altar at Gibeon, he was playing his role as the nation's chief executive officer, not as a man of God. He found it more convenient to celebrate civil religion than to proclaim God's prophetic judgment against idolatry. In fact, Solomon had probably grown so accustomed to what he was doing that it no longer even seemed like idolatry to him. He was simply performing according to cultural custom.

Christians in the marketplace can identify with Solomon's dilemma. Virtually everyone is confronted by compromises dictated by professional etiquette and cultural custom, whether we are lawyers or doctors, nurses or salespeople. It may be as simple as being told at Rotary not to conclude your prayer "in Jesus' name" because it may offend fellow Rotarians who belong to "other faiths." Or it may be as complex as your boss asking you to juggle the accounting figures to make things look better than they really are. It may be the pressure to play along with your flirtatious colleague so you will be accepted.

Or it may mean living according to the same standard of living as your professional peers, even though that standard may be excessive and self-indulgent. It may mean working seven days a week to get the job done because that is what it takes to get ahead. It may mean performing abortions, neglecting the poor, building nuclear bombs, selling pornographic magazines, upholding client advocacy no matter what, or pretending at opportune moments not to know Christ. Are we so different from Solomon? Do we get in our cars on Monday morning and drive to our Gibeons to sacrifice our time, energy, emotional drive, and spiritual commitment to our cultural idols?

The Dialogue of the Soul

Solomon's home was in Jerusalem, but that is not, where God spoke to him. In the middle of the night, after Solomon had had a busy day with matters of protocol and public relations, God came to him at Gibeon. Of all places for God to speak to Solomon, Gibeon seems the most unlikely. Yet it was here, after a full day of compromise and appeasement, that Solomon experienced the decision of his lifetime. In the quiet of the night, in the deep recesses of his consciousness, Solomon heard God's invitation to receive what all the goodwill of Gibeon could not give him: "Ask for whatever you want me to give you" (1 Kings 3:5).

It was in Gibeon that Solomon proved himself by his request. But the more important fact is that God took the initiative to encounter Solomon in Gibeon and provide him with a fresh opportunity. The question of whether we want an educated heart comes in the midst of a marketplace of ideas and lifestyles, where we are surrounded by the strategies and priorities of making it in the real world. God breaks in and asks the soul-searching question. We may mistake this spiritual inquiry as an overactive mind after a hectic day, but it is God's merciful interrogation of the soul, which if responded to effectively, integrates the depth of our personal being with our public actions. The real challenge Solomon faced came in the middle of the night when he was alone with God. That special night was prime time for testing the wisdom of his heart.

Solomon celebrated his spiritual success by hastening back to Jerusalem to stand before the "ark of the Lord's covenant." He sealed that late-night spiritual resolution, with its profound ethical implications, by returning to Jerusalem to worship the Lord. He demonstrated his heart's commitment devotionally by offering sacrifices to God and relationally by giving a feast for his court. Solomon was a happy man. He had caught a glimpse of what God could do for him and through him.

All Truth Is God's Truth

The scope of God's wisdom became evident in Solomon's life. We are told that "God gave Solomon wisdom and very great insight, and a breadth of understanding as measureless as the sand on the seashore" (1 Kings 4:29). He was the wisest man of the East. Intellectuals from all over journeyed to Solomon's court to discuss everything from music to agriculture. He excelled in poetry, music, botany, and zoology. He was exceptionally endowed by God with both artistic creativity and analytical skills.

In an age of specialists such as ours it may be difficult to appreciate the comprehensiveness of Solomon's knowledge. Our academic communities train people to be experts in their particular fields. Knowledge is categorized and compartmentalized. Rarely do we find people today who have a comprehensive knowledge of many things. Today's educational goal is usually a specialized knowledge of some particular matter. Solomon was different. His stated request for discernment was not divorced from embracing the totality of God's creation, from reflecting on human nature to researching a rare sea creature.

Solomon's example is instructive for several reasons. Those who share his desire for a discerning heart must not minimize God's creation by disparaging intellectual competence. Wisdom and knowledge ought to go hand-in-hand. An educated heart is not contrary to an education in the arts and sciences. Wherever we find truth we find God's truth. Academic pursuits apart from ethical sensitivity and the divine moral order lose their intended human purpose. They may end up working against, rather than for, mankind. But how misguided it would be to place intelligence and morality in opposition. The Christian mind is not out of place in the university. Those who strive to understand and willingly submit to God's moral will are those who ought to be excited about exploring every facet of the universe for the glory of God.

I have met brilliant people whose lives were in moral disarray. The problem was not their intelligence, although it may have bolstered their pride, but their foolishness. Such people have a great deal to offer. They look at world affairs and analyze current events perceptively. They delve into the deep recesses of the human imagination and canvass sociological trends with precision. They examine the outer reaches of the galaxy and invent new technologies. Yet they are foolish. They refuse to accept and appreciate the Author of life. They are cosmic orphans, come of age, without a home. One minute they think they are masters of the universe; the next moment they feel estranged from everything and everyone. Solomon's model does not sacrifice intelligence for morality but neither does it sacrifice morality for intelligence. True wisdom is indivisible, integrating all aspects of truth into one life-related whole.

The Pursuit of Excellence

Solomon was not only a brilliant academician, he was also a preeminent administrator. The Queen of Sheba was overwhelmed with Solomon's court. Everything surrounding Solomon appeared exquisitely managed. From the caliber of advisors and gourmet food to palace protocol and temple worship, Solomon personified the pursuit of excellence. The Queen of Sheba was amazed and astounded. She found it nearly unbelievable. She spoke with wonder about the great joy it must have been for Solomon's servants to serve in his court (1 Kings 10:8). It sounds exaggerated, I know, but that was her assessment of the work environment created by Solomon.

In this, too, Solomon models a quality of work and an attention to detail implied in a discerning heart. We have no indication in the biblical text that Solomon's early administration had become a source of sinful extravagance and waste. The wisdom of God is not divorced from the practical affairs of financial management, time schedules, a healthy diet, proper attire, and efficiency. The simple fact that Solomon, a recipient of God's wisdom, excelled in these areas challenges the indifference some Christians feel toward these matters. They may talk about justice and ethical sensitivity, but when it comes to daily efforts, they waste their energies through disorganization and mismanagement.

Some may be tempted to use Solomon's lifestyle to defend excessive spending and to legitimize a gospel of health and wealth. This would be a grave mistake. The practical wisdom displayed in Solomon's court should not be used to justify financial mismanagement and self-indulgence. What impressed the Queen of Sheba was the wisdom of Solomon's administration not his posh surroundings. The intellectual, spiritual, and relational climate of Solomon's court led this foreign dignitary to honor the God of Solomon: "Praise be to the LORD your God, who has delighted in you and placed you on the throne of Israel. Because of the LORD's eternal love for Israel, he has made you king, to maintain justice and righteousness" (1 Kings 10:9).

The queen observed that God had made Solomon king for a purpose. The moral order of his administration was intended to maintain justice and righteousness. Solomon's wisdom was for the sake of social justice. All of his intellectual and managerial skills were given to him by God to fulfill his request for a discerning heart. Solomon's wisdom shines intellectually and administratively; but the fundamental quality of his wisdom was the pursuit of justice.

Justice

Immediately following the account of Solomon's celebration in Jerusalem, we are given an example of his wisdom (1 Kings 3:16–28). Solomon had asked for and received a discerning heart; now the narrative proceeds to illustrate the character of "a wise and discerning heart."

Wisdom is not left in the abstract. It is demonstrated in an unusual test case. An examination of this well-known case study will reveal that wisdom's high calling is justice. Ultimate importance is given to putting things right.

Two women came before Solomon; one claimed that the other had stolen her baby in the middle of the night while she slept. They were prostitutes living by themselves in the same house, nursing their babies who were only a few days old. One claimed the other accidentally suffocated her own baby by lying on him. This other woman then exchanged her dead baby for the living baby asleep at his mother's side. In the morning she awoke to find the other woman's dead baby at her breast.

It would be difficult to find a more emotionally charged issue. One woman's baby has died and the other woman's baby has been stolen. Both women are painfully threatened in the depths of their being. It would also be difficult to find a more impossible case to solve. Without blood tests and supporting witnesses the truth is locked up in the soul. Who is telling the truth? Has one women accidentally smothered her child and frantically stolen another, or has the other woman deviously devised to use the judicial system to gain an innocent woman's child through false accusation because her own child died?

As challenging as the case may be, we marvel that Solomon heard the case at all. The two women standing before him were prostitutes. This helps explain their housing situation and how they came to be sleeping alone with their two babies. It also tells us that they were poor. Prostitutes were usually slaves, who had been sold by their destitute parents. They may never have had the opportunity to marry. Yet the description bears more significance than that they were poor.

In the book of Proverbs a prostitute personifies evil and foolishness. She represents the seduction of evil, the sensual antithesis to everything wisdom stands for. With these two women designated as prostitutes, we learn more than an added circumstantial detail. We learn that the pursuit of justice takes place in the midst of systemic evil. The society in which we seek to put things right is evil through and through. Its evil is deep-rooted and complex, intertwined in all human affairs.

Let me try to illustrate what I mean by structural evil. The land our home is on was once part of a farm. The backyard is surrounded by a chain-link fence running along the property line. About ten feet inside the fence is a dense growth of bushes, vines, and trees. When I attempted to clear a path through the growth, I discovered the farm's old barbed wire fence. The trees had grown up around it and through it and some instances the barbed wire was deeply imbedded in the trees and bushes. From a few feet away you could hardly see it, but it was there and had to come down so my children would not run into it when they played. Removing the barbed wire took longer than I anticipated.

The fence was so intertwined with the brush and trees that I had to spend hours cutting through the barbed wire with a hacksaw, slowly extracting the fence from its nearly invisible stranglehold on the trees. That barbed-wire fence is a picture for me of the evil in our society that is deeply embedded in and wrapped around the way we do business, how we think about ourselves, how we relate sexually, how we act politically. Life has grown up around and through this evil, which has a stranglehold on how life is lived. The evil does not come down by cutting into it at one point.

In itself evil can become an excuse for not dealing with evil. Solomon could have refused to hear the women's case simply because he was having to deal with two prostitutes. He could have used their evil ways to excuse his inattentiveness to their plea for justice. Would a moralist be able to see past the immoral lifestyle of these two women and deal with human injustice? Violence by blacks in South Africa is an excuse used by many who refuse to support the cause of justice in that land. Homosexual practice by some who contract AIDS is used as a justification for limiting medical resources in the fight against AIDS. Many right-wing propagandists have learned that the quickest way to kill support for civil rights and minority rights is to spread the rumor that the advocates for justice are communist sympathizers. Even the hint of evil becomes an excuse for sinfully neglecting the cause of justice.

There is no denying that these two women were living contrary to the will of God. Understanding the complexity of systemic evil does not, however, remove their personal guilt and responsibility for their lifestyle. Nor, at the same time, can it be used to deny them justice. A prostitute appealed to Solomon for justice and he heard her case. Why did this woman deserve the king's judicial decision? Obviously she possessed no power or position of importance; yet it does not seem unusual in the biblical account for the king to have heard this poor sinful woman's plea.

We can imagine other reactions: "Let them work it out between themselves. It's their problem, not the king's problem!" Or, "Who really cares about the child anyway? One mother is as good or as bad as the other!"

The American *Declaration of Independence* reads, "We hold these truths to be self-evident, that all men are created equal and endowed with certain inalienable rights: life, liberty and the pursuit of happiness." What rights were "self-evident" for this distraught woman who claimed her child had been stolen? What were the grounds for her appeal for justice? How does the secularist or the materialist explain the "self-evident" quality of her "inalienable rights"?

Justice does not depend on the woman's social standing. If it did, society surely would have found a reason for denying her access to Solomon's court. She does not merit just arbitration through her inherent goodness and respectability. And she certainly did not have the strength and power to demand it. Like the unborn child, the mentally underdeveloped, and the poor, this woman had an inherent right to justice because she was made in the image of God. She was made "a little lower than the heavenly beings and crowned . . . with glory and honor" (Ps. 8:5).

As the psalmist declared, "I know that the Lord secures justice for the poor and upholds the cause of the needy" (140:12). She had a right to justice because God had given her that right. Society can always find reasons for not giving people justice, but those reasons run counter to God's moral order.

The assumptions surrounding this case bear significant testimony to the biblical understanding of man. The fundamental conviction that the human person is made in the image of God influenced Hebrew culture practically and shaped the responsibility of the king. Solomon did not excuse himself from this case on the grounds that he had more important things to do than deal with two poor prostitutes. He did not avoid the high calling of setting things right for the needy; that was his duty before the God of Israel. He heard the case because it was important to God. He pursued justice for the sake of God's kingdom. Solomon reasoned that if a person has a God-given right, the king has a duty to honor it.

The hard work of solving moral problems in the real world involves dealing with people and issues we would like to ignore. It would be easier if we could pass off the responsibility to someone else. But Solomon could not refuse the plea for justice and remain faithful to his God-given commission and neither can we. The words of Moses need to ring in our ears; "Follow justice and justice alone, so that you may live" (Deut. 16:20). We are offered this challenge in every sphere of life, in the lives we live as parents, students, professionals, citizens, pastors, farmers, laborers, grandparents, missionaries, salesclerks, and friends.

One night I was standing at the kitchen sink doing the dishes when I overheard my boys arguing outside. I was tired, and hearing them argue was too much after a long day at work. I burst out the back door ready to vent my frustration when I remembered Solomon. I am glad that the moral force of the Bible comes to bear at such a time as that. I stopped in my anger and realized I needed to take the time to arbitrate, to put things right. I needed to take the time to hear each side and to work for justice right there on the driveway with my two boys.

As a pastor, I ought to be trying to put things right. That does not mean appeasing all sides. It does not mean making everyone happy. It means pursuing justice even when it would be so much easier and expedient to ignore the injustices. Compassion and reconciliation are time-consuming, energy-draining, frequently frustrating endeavors, but that is what biblical wisdom is all about. "He has showed you, O man, what is good," declared the prophet Micah. "And what does the LORD require of you? To act justly and to love mercy and to walk humbly with your God" (Micah 6:8).

We cannot have righteousness without justice, even if that is what moralists want, nor can we have justice without righteousness, no matter how zealous our political activism. Biblical justice and true righteousness are inseparable. We cannot have one without the other. When politicians call for justice and live immorally they reveal their evil character. When fundamentalists call for evangelism yet live selfish, indulgent lives they expose their evil character. Moral order consists of social justice and personal holiness. Together they comprise righteous character and just action.

We need to see Solomon's test case from three perspectives: that of the innocent woman who desperately pleads for her son, that of the king who bears the responsibility to seek justice for the weak and powerless, and that of the woman who has stolen the child to replace her dead son. The third angle requires some special consideration.

The report we have of how the child died was given by the woman who brought the case: "During the night this woman's son died because she lay on him" (1 Kings 3:19). The child may or may not have died this way. There is no proof. The child may have died of "crib death." Now, imagine yourself waking up to find your child dead.

Suddenly you are dealt a crushing blow. You are hammered by fear and anger, smashed by grief and guilt. You grope about in pain. What do you do when you are victimized by evil? How do you respond when your life is catastrophically changed by an evil beyond your control?

I am afraid we often do what this woman did. She lashed out, and so do we. Since life had dealt her a cruel blow, she fought back. She did the unthinkable. She took another woman's child. Because she had been hurt, she hurt someone else. She had to even the score and protect herself. Her pain became another's pain. One way or another she was going to make it. She was a survivalist. Undoubtedly she felt forced into doing what she did. She could not bear to face the evil, so she attempted to live a lie. Evil enticed her to choose between her dead son and another woman's live son; she chose the other woman's son. She chose death instead of life. She sought to overcome the evil with evil. We see ourselves in this woman. Sinful human nature fights against evil with the weapons of the world: deception, violence, greed, malice, and self-glory. Evil is a vicious circle consuming the soul and destroying the world.

Moral Risk-Taking

Something must be done to put things right. But what can be done? A decision must be reached, a course of action followed. The truth must be discovered, but how? After Solomon summarized the case, he did what no one would have dreamed of. He ordered a sword and commanded that the living child be slashed in half. Suddenly the picture of our enlightened monarch, intelligent and urbane, crumbles. We seem suddenly to enter the world of ruthless power and arbitrary cruelty. Is this how justice is pursued?

The pursuit of justice is not for the fainthearted. What appears at first reading to be cruel and unusual is actually daring. Solomon knew that the truth must be obtained indirectly. No amount of direct questioning would detect the lie. His strategy had all the appearance of that of a tyrant impatient with a no-win case. Kill the child and be done with it. The moralist might in fact argue that this verdict was just, seeing that both women were prostitutes. Thankfully, however, the case study continues. What appeared on the surface to be arbitrary and cruel was actually a brilliant and creative move that boldly set up the moment of truth. Like a skilled surgeon, who knows a life hangs in the balance, Solomon confidently cuts to the truth. In his hand he holds a scalpel, not a weapon. He goes to the life-threatening edge to pursue justice.

Solomon's risk-taking depended on the moral sensitivity of the innocent mother. Just when she had given her all, more was demanded of her. We feel the agony of the moment as this woman desperately sought the life of her son. Her pursuit of justice could not have been more personal, more heart-wrenching. Every ounce of emotional energy was expended to make her plea and win back her son. But after she had made her case for justice, she was asked for something more. Solomon's strategy demanded from her a painful, almost unthinkable decision. Her moral conscience took her beyond her maternal rights and guided her love toward the ultimate sacrifice. The indirect quest for truth carried an obvious painful necessity for her. She had to give up her son to the evil woman to save his life. She had no time for rage. She came seeking justice; now she must give up her right to justice. She had the moral sense, the brave resolve, to give up her child to let him live. When she cried out spontaneously, "Please, my lord, give her the living baby! Don't kill him!" the suspense was broken, the truth known. The true love of the real mother emerged from the painful, moral sensitivity of the innocent woman. The hard-won verdict was easy. Solomon only needed to state the obvious: "Give the living baby to the first woman. Do not kill him; she is his mother" (1 Kings 3:27).

Of all the things that Solomon accomplished in his

career, pursuing justice was what impressed people the most. "When all Israel heard the verdict the king had given, they held the king in awe, because they saw that he had wisdom from God to administer justice" (1 Kings 3:28).

People really do find justice awesome. The grandeur of Solomon's court and the brilliance of his intellect were secondary to his pursuit of justice. Solomon was respected for many things, but his ability to administer justice stood above all other considerations. Justice inspired the community. It gave them confidence in his leadership. As long as justice was Solomon's trademark, he had the people's respect. He was worthy to lead because he evidenced the wisdom of God. It may appear that people are attracted to the lives of the rich and famous, to the glitter of celebrity status; but when it comes down to it, the person of character who seeks justice is the man or woman held in high esteem.

The Ethic of the Cross

One final word needs to be said about Solomon's pursuit of justice and the moral capacity and compassion of the innocent woman. At the heart of this story we see the principle of the Cross, "my life for yours," dramatically illustrated. Like Solomon, God was a moral risk taker. God was willing to lay it all on the line to gain justice. He sent his Son to the cross to bear the just penalty for our sin. Solomon's absurd threat—divide the child in half—compares with the absurdity of the Cross. How can justice be gained by the death of an innocent man? But it was precisely at this point of absurdity that the wisdom of God is revealed. The Cross exposed evil and revealed the love of God for us. The truth about our sinful selves and God's verdict against all evil became powerfully clear.

Like the woman who gave up her right to her son, the Father gave up his Son that we might live. Out of compassion she was willing to do the unthinkable. God did the unthinkable. He went to the cross and died for us. He pursued justice with a holy sacrifice. He took upon himself the evil absurdity that we might live.

There is no other foundation for the educated heart than the experience of the Cross. The bond between ourselves and God is forged out of his great love for us. Against every form of conventional wisdom that endeavors to work life out through moralistic platitudes and pleasure-seeking conveniences, God reminds us of the seriousness of our moral need and the price God paid to restore us to a life of moral order and purpose. Such a life can never be the result of our own achievement. It is God who establishes moral order in our life through the life, death, and resurrection of the One who is greater than Solomon.

QUESTIONS FOR DISCUSSION

1. How does Solomon's cultural situation compare to your own? Do you agree that the Word of God can speak to you and move you beyond the habits of the heart reflected in the moral status quo of your culture?
2. What does the scope of Solomon's wisdom teach us about God's wisdom?
3. Do you agree that true wisdom is manifested not only in moral discernment and righteous action but also in a broad range of intellectual pursuits and practical concerns?
4. Why is it remarkable that Solomon heard the case between these two women? What were the qualities of Israel's culture that contributed to Solomon's involvement?
5. Do you agree that all Christians should be involved in pursuing justice and setting things right? What special opportunities do you have to seek justice because of your family, work, and social responsibilities?
6. What did Solomon's moral risk-taking depend on?
7. Do you agree that the ultimate pursuit of justice led to the cross of Jesus?

8

Moral Endurance

The tragedy of Solomon's life is that what began so well ended so poorly. In his early years as king, Solomon modeled the character of an educated heart. In his later years, his decadent life became a pitiful warning. His story began with a simple request for wisdom and humble dependence on God. He felt the burden of his royal responsibilities and approached his task with a servant's heart. He administered the kingdom in a way that brought joy to his servants. His youthful enthusiasm demonstrated a heart for God and compassion and respect for the people. He pursued justice boldly and creatively. He was intent on following in the wisdom and spirituality of his father David. He sought to fulfill his father's dream by building a temple to the glory of God. All in all, Solomon's early life combined a passion for God with a brilliant quest for learning, administrative excellence, and an unbiased pursuit of social justice.

Sad to say, it would have been better if Solomon's life had ended when he was still in his spiritual prime. His moral life disintegrated under the pressure of personal ambition, sexual fixation, and power addiction. The one who began as such a moral contrast to Absalom eventually went beyond Absalom in self-indulgence. His earlier intolerance of injustice and spiritual infidelity evolved into a blatant tolerance of poverty, polygamy, idolatry, and spiritual apathy. Instead of being a servant to God's people he became an oppressor, exploiting the labor and livelihood of the poor.

The wealth of the land and the fruit of God's blessing flowed to Jerusalem for costly building projects and lavish displays of opulence. Solomon sat on an ivory throne overlaid by fine gold and adorned with twelve golden lions. His throne bore the mark of distinction sought by all self-indulgent materialists: "Nothing like it had ever been made for any other kingdom" (1 Kings 10:20). The distinctive nature of the Hebrew people envisioned by Moses, Joshua, Samuel, and David was lost under the status-seeking aspirations of Solomon. The "greatness" of Solomon was no longer measured by his faithfulness to the Law of God but by his world-renowned accumulations of horses, chariots, gold, and women.

Solomon's love affair with the world was most evident in his obsession with sexual satisfaction. His seven hundred foreign wives and three hundred concubines turned his heart away from the Lord. He shamelessly built shrines to fertility goddesses and erected altars to burn children as a sacrifice to the idol Molech. It is conceivable that some of Solomon's own children were prized sacrifices offered in these cult rituals.

The spiritual apathy and moral degeneracy of Solomon's later years seem to exceed the worst possible scenario. He might as well have been the king of Babylon as the king of Israel. How could a man of moral character and wisdom change so radically? Solomon's decline teaches us not to underestimate the power of conspicuous consumption, sensual pleasure, and self-indulgence to undermine the educated heart. No matter who we are, "centering life in the insatiable demands of the ego is the sure path to doom."[1]

If Solomon with all of his wisdom could fall, so can we. He is a sober warning to the faithful and an easy excuse for the disobedient. Age is no guarantee for spiritual insight and ethical wisdom. Growing old does not of itself make one wiser or more obedient. In fact it may provide the excuse for giving up what wisdom one does have in exchange for selfish pleasure and moral indifference. The older Solomon became, the more he despised his single-minded devotion to God. In place of worship he substituted success; instead of justice he gave himself to indulgence. He replaced spirituality with lust, and compassion with conceit. Solomon ruined his life by running around in a maze of enticements, seductions, and excesses. He started out on the path of obedience but lost his way en route. What began in grace ended in disgrace.

Chasing the Wind

Solomon's moral decline was gradual, spread over years of striving for personal fulfillment. The simple, passionate faith of his father David was interrogated and challenged by his son's intense quest for meaning. Solomon gave the habits of the heart full range of expression. He wanted to see what was worthwhile for men to do under heaven during the few days of their lives. So he acquired

[1]Eugene Peterson, *Earth and Altar: The Community of Prayer in a Self-Bound Society* (Downers Grove, Ill., InterVarsity, 1985), p. 21.

knowledge, experienced pleasure, undertook great projects, and amassed wealth. He explored the limits of money, sex, and power. He denied himself nothing he desired and refused his heart no pleasure. Yet when he surveyed all that he had done and what he had labored to achieve, "everything was meaningless, a chasing after the wind; nothing was gained under the sun" (Eccl. 2:11).

In his later years Solomon epitomizes the life that is lost in the living. In his quest to make life easy he only made it more difficult. His comfort zones had become cubicles of loneliness and despair. He was a prisoner in the world of his own making. The difference between Solomon's frantic effort and the striving of many today may be only in the intensity of the quest. Solomon had the intellectual capacity and financial means to test the limits of hedonism. The magnitude of his projects and the extent of his self-indulgence may exceed the resources of many, but not their dreams. They share the same temptations, the same habits of the heart. Like Solomon, they struggle for many things that are meaningless. Instead of long obedience in the same direction they become sidetracked and are caught in the rat race. Their striving for success and intimacy may be subtler than Solomon's but no less real and absorbing.

The struggles of some Christians can be likened to running in a maze. Like the white mice in the psychologist's experiment, people are running around frantically in a moral maze of confusion. They run in and out of cubicles marked education, marriage, careers, leisure, without any sense of purpose or direction. They have no horizon of understanding or moral vision. In their effort to gain success, self-esteem, companionship, and peace of mind, they do what Solomon did. They gradually deny their moral and spiritual character for the sake of immediate gratification and self-comfort. The imperial self rules out simple devotion, the rhythm of worship and prayer, the spontaneity of praise, and the expressions of gratitude. Like Solomon, they go the way of the surrounding culture. The well-publicized habits of the heart separate knowledge from wisdom, pleasure from moral virtue, and success from service.

Wrong-headed Activism

The solution to this maze of moral confusion is not found in extending the maze. Well-intentioned but misguided Christians attack the frustration of the maze by adding more cubicles. They moralize the maze. They construct cubicles to religious pride and a legalistic code of conduct. They run through sports mania into capitalistic zeal. Then they turn right into Bible memorization and left into antisecular humanism. They have cubicles dedicated to Christian colleges, seminars, and denominations. Life in the religious maze is programed in a sequence of steps of indoctrination designed to guide a Christian past the dangerous cubicles of relativism and secularism. But the maze is still a maze. The same bigotry and bitterness characterize both the moralist and the secularist. There is no horizon of moral perception, no vision of inner character strength. The imperial self, whether secularized or moralized, is left to wander through the maze in happy oblivion or frustrated fatigue.

Much of today's Christian activism is wrong-headed and reflects the mindless mentality of the maze. It subjects the Christian life to fits and spurts, bursts of zeal without wisdom, activism barren of biblical insight, high-tech evangelism wanting for body-life, and spiritual hype insensitive to the complexity of evil. Christians are running out of energy in getting from one cubicle to another. They are burning out and dropping out. They are caught in a performance trap that leaves them wasted. Those who are rushing around in the religious maze are no longer certain of what they want out of life. They are unable to distinguish between willing obedience and willfulness, between false guilt and Spirit-led action, between self-expression and self-denial.

Wrong-headed activism means imposing our will on God's work. It is often an expression of our pent up frustration with life. We take advantage of a situation by venting our self-serving indignation. It was right for Moses to be angry with the disobedience of the Israelites at Kadesh. But it was wrong for Moses to allow his anger to control his actions. Instead of speaking to the rock, he struck the rock. The water gushed out and the people drank, but Moses was judged: "Because you did not trust in me enough to honor me as holy in the sight of the Israelites, you will not bring this community into the land I give them" (Num. 20:12). God's sensitivity to Moses' disobedience manifests a concern both for the means as well as the end. God is unwilling to have his authority usurped, even by the leader of his own choosing acting on his behalf. No issue or cause justifies violating God's expressed will. We are not to be overcome by evil the way Moses was, who used the occasion to vent his own anger and frustration. But we are to overcome evil with good.

Fear and insecurity are also catalysts for wrong-headed activism. A key incident in King Saul's life illustrates this well (1 Sam. 13:1–15). When Saul and the army of Israel were besieged by the Philistines, Saul felt compelled to assume the responsibilities of Samuel. The army was beginning to scatter and the appointed time for Samuel's arrival had passed; so in a desperate effort to boost morale and prepare for war, Saul offered sacrifices and burnt offerings. Driven by fear, Saul presumptuously went ahead of God's command and performed the duties reserved for a priest. He used an act of worship to maintain his authority and serve his political ends. Given the situation it seemed like the only thing he could do. But it was the wrong thing. Instead of waiting for Samuel, he felt compelled by fear to offer the sacrifices.

Like Saul, the misguided activist feels that the necessity of the moment justifies a small abuse for a greater good. It may involve a slight misrepresentation to raise funds for a good cause, or it may lead to manipulating a worship service to gain personal support. In the case of Saul, this seemingly small indiscretion proved momentous. He lost the kingdom. God could no longer trust him. In a moment of crisis, fear drove out faithfulness, and wrong-headed activism stepped in to rescue self-confidence and wounded pride.

Another prominent prod to wrong-headed activism is an ego-gratifying display of heroism. The original team of Jesus' disciples offers numerous examples of moral confusion and wrong-headed activism. For instance, James and John wanted to call down fire from heaven to destroy a Samaritan village; on another occasion, the disciples were prepared to send away thousands of hungry people (Luke 9:54; Matt. 14:15). What the disciples wanted to do may have vented their anger or alleviated the immediate problem, but their intent ran roughshod over the will of Jesus. Peter was especially prone to react out of his own willfulness, even to the point of rebuking the Lord he had just confessed. One moment he testified, "You are the Christ, the Son of the Living God"; the next moment, when Jesus spoke of his imminent suffering and death, he censured Jesus, "Never, Lord! This shall never happen to you!" (Matt. 16:16, 22).

Peter's inclination toward heroism was displayed on the night Jesus was arrested. As the temple guards approached Jesus to arrest him, Peter drew his sword and lunged toward the high priest's servant, cutting off his ear. In the midst of the confusion Jesus stopped everything, healed the man's ear, and reprimanded his willful disciple. He had to undo the damage perpetrated by one of his own disciples (Luke 22:50–51). Like many Christians today, Peter felt he had to do something. He had to stand up and be counted. He had to prove his loyalty. But a few hours later that evening, when he was asked by a young girl if he had been with Jesus, he angrily denied ever knowing him (Matt. 26:69–75).

When social action is the product of self-serving indignation or a fear-induced compulsion or a willful display of heroism, the will and work of God are not served. Moses, Saul and Peter may have been well-meaning activists who sincerely felt they were doing God a favor, but they failed to understand the essence of God's work. Their efforts were the product of the religious maze. They refused to wait and raced ahead of God. They took the initiative and sought to control the situation. At a critical point each turned the ethical challenge into an opportunity of self-expression. They did not seek God's will but their own.

Out of the Maze

Solomon's quest for success and satisfaction ended in failure. We can hear his despair as he intones, " 'Meaningless! Meaningless!' says the Teacher. 'Utterly meaningless! Everything is meaningless' " (Eccl. 1:1). His life, a picture of sinful excess and moral disarray, serves as a warning to all who impose their own will on the life God has given them. The message of Ecclesiastes, however, is not despair but hope. There is a way out of the maze, a road right out of self. The art of living is not left to our own imagination and striving. It involves abandoning the self-absorbed "calculus of inner needs" and receiving the grace of God. Life is a gift from God to be enjoyed in simple accord and singular devotion to the Author of life.

Social analyst Daniel Yankelovich notes an important truth that many who run in the maze fail to see. "By concentrating day and night on your feelings, potentials, needs, and wants, and desires, and by learning to assert them more freely, you do not become a freer, more spontaneous, more creative self; you become a narrower, more self-centered, more isolated one. You do not grow, you shrink."[2] Instead of a moral duty to self, we have a moral duty to our Creator. Life is not left to our own

[2] Daniel Yankelovich, *New Rules: Searching for Self-Fulfillment in a World Turned Upside Down* (New York: Bantam Books, 1982), p. 239.

initiative and achievement but to our obedience and prayer. God's grace precedes forgiving and blessing.

The maze of moral confusion ends where the educated heart begins. The fear of God establishes the ethic behind our ethics. We begin not with a list of controversial issues but with a life commitment to the One greater than Solomon. Moral-order living is not complicated or ingenious. Throughout the Word of God it is simply stated. We enter into a life of prayer and thanksgiving "that we may live peaceful and quiet lives in all godliness and holiness. This is good," commends the apostle Paul, "and pleases God our Savior, who wants all men to be saved and to come to a knowledge of the truth" (1 Tim. 2:1–4). We make it our "ambition to lead a quiet life," to mind our own business and to work diligently, "so that [our] daily life may win the respect of outsiders and so that [we] will not be dependent on anybody" (1 Thess. 4:11–12). It means overcoming evil with good and offering our lives as living sacrifices, holy and pleasing to God, which is our sensible service (Rom. 12:1–2, 21). The educated heart sets apart Christ as Lord and is prepared to answer everyone who asks the reason for Christian hope. The Christian response, both ethically and evangelistically, is gentle and respectful so that those who speak maliciously against "good behavior in Christ may be ashamed of their slander" (1 Peter 3:15–16).

Moral-order living does not compartmentalize life into cubicles, each with a specialized ethic. A Christian ethic provides a unified field theory of moral reflection and action. The ethic behind the ethics comprehends a myriad decisions and concerns, each answered in reference to the fear of God, not man; the lordship of Christ, not self; the whole counsel of God, not the opinions of man; the ethic of the Cross, not the expediency of the moment. A Christian ethic makes sense. "We do not learn our relationship with God out of a cocksure knowledge of exactly what God wants, which then launches us into a vigorous clean-up campaign of the world on his behalf. . . ."[3] Real faith in God is essentially practical not promotional. It requires humility not publicity. "Religion that God our Father accepts as pure and faultless is this: to look after orphans and widows in their distress and to keep oneself from being polluted by the world" (James 1:27). Moral-order living understands humble service, inner strength, quiet resolve, disciplined growth, and the sacrifice of praise. It is in the routine of life, at the center of our daily existence with all its tensions and tedium, that the educated heart pulsates with grace and truth.

Into the Marathon

Escaping the maze and entering the marathon is the most freeing thing that can happen in a person's life. Instead of running around in a maze of moralistic self-righteousness or in a maze of relativistic self-pleasure, we are free to "run with perseverance the race marked out for us" (Heb. 12:1).

"God made me fast, and when I run I feel his favor" was the way Eric Liddell expressed his reason for entering the 1924 Olympics. It is easy to remember that sense of exhilaration, seeing Eric Liddell cross the finish line in *Chariots of Fire*, winning the gold medal. He committed several years of his life and threw himself into preparing for the Paris games. He invested his time and energy into running the Olympic race. And when he won, the race was over. He knew what he had to do, and he did it. He had achieved his goal.

In life we long for that moment of exhilarating release when we have accomplished a long-sought goal—when we can say it is finished. But the ethical challenge Christians face is not like a 400-meter race. It requires more than a quick burst of spiritual energy in college or the moral enthusiasm generated by a single ethical issue. The mara-

[3]Eugene Peterson, "Growth: An Act of the Will?" *Leadership* (Fall 1988), p. 40.

thon God has entered us in is not a relay race where we can pass the baton of moral responsibility to another runner.

When it comes to illustrating the Christian character and moral endurance, Canadian runner Terry Fox comes to mind. His trek across Canada is a more appropriate picture of the perseverance required to face the ethical challenge than Eric Liddell's Olympic sprint. Terry Fox died from cancer in 1981, but not before inspiring a nation with his personal courage. Setting out to jog across Canada on an artificial limb, he became a symbol of hope and persever-ance. His quest came to be called the Marathon of Hope. Terry Fox succeeded in raising millions of dollars for cancer research but even more important and impossible to measure was the impact of his determination on millions of Canadians. Terry Fox's marathon was not over until his life was over. That is how it is with the Christian.

Although Terry Fox's marathon of hope may be a better analogy of the Christian life than Eric Liddell's 400-meter race, Liddell's life stands as a great example of spiritual stamina and moral endurance. He obeyed the call of God to go to China as a missionary where he served until his death. His life did not peak at the 1924 Olympics. He saw Jesus leading him to China for a life of service and hardship far more demanding than the Olympics. Eric Liddell put the events that made him famous behind him and ran the marathon of faith with his eyes fixed on Jesus. Liddell won that race, too, and proved that the educated heart is a lifetime commitment.

Marathons are by their very nature endurance tests. They do not televise well. The runner runs mile after mile of even-paced running. No home runs, no touchdowns, no slam-dunks, no point scores; in fact, there is not even a ball in play. We may enter the race with visions of half-time highlights from ABC's Monday Night Football, but we are faced with an exhausting, sometimes lonely, mile-after-mile struggle. It is easy to have second thoughts and wish that somebody else was running in our place. We might even wish that the moral marathon were a spectator sport.

Spiritual couch potatoes run poorly. A diet rich in pop Christianity provides little energy for the uphill stretches. Those who thrive on emotional fluff and felt-need attention stop running when the cheering stops and the rain begins. Exercise workouts are optional. The practice of prayer, confession, worship, and Bible study is inconsistent. There is no rhythm to Christian fellowship or commitment to the Sabbath principle. The spiritual disciplines have never been internalized. They remain external to the soul—techniques that may come in handy if willpower fails and enthusiasm wanes.

The moral marathoner runs without the burden of extra baggage. She is not possessed by her possessions or weighed down by an inflated ego. She is not so wrapped up with herself that she cannot concentrate on the race. The distractions of her past are laid aside. She throws off the hindrances of insecurity, perfectionism, and moodiness and refuses to allow her ethic to get tangled up in job security and career advancement.

The race is clearly marked out for us. If we take a wrong turn and end up in a maze of side streets and back alleys, it's because our eyes are not fixed on Jesus, the author and perfecter of our faith. The Christian was never meant to run alone. We may not be cheered on by an admiring audience, but we are accompanied by a great team of spiritual marathoners urging us on and setting the pace. The writer of Hebrews wished to convince the followers of Jesus that they never run alone. We belong to a long history of marathoners, one of whom was Moses, who "regarded disgrace for the sake of Christ as of greater value than the treasures of Egypt" (Heb. 11:26).

The most significant runner in our field of vision is Jesus. The Solomons of the world may run brilliantly for a time, but they eventually drop out. The author and perfecter of our faith keeps up the pace. His energy becomes our strength and his knowledge of the course our confidence. We run the marathon with our eyes fixed on Jesus. His faithfulness is the ground for our faith, his path to the cross not only the means of our salvation but also the model for our ethic. His victory over sin and death is our victory, and his bodily resurrection the promise of our own.

We run the race not on a political platform of single issues or moralistic platitudes. We run not out of fear or pride or frustration. We are not running scared. We are not running away because the world threatens to overwhelm us. We are running strong and free, on a path that leads to glory. We are running with our eyes fixed on Jesus, "who for the joy set before him endured the cross, scorning its shame, and sat down at the right hand of the throne of God" (Heb. 12:2). Those who run in the maze will sooner or later conclude with the writer of Ecclesiastes: "When I surveyed all that my hands had done and what I had toiled to achieve, everything was meaningless, a chasing after the wind; nothing was gained under the sun" (2:11).

That is the end of the maze. But for those who run the marathon, an eternity of exhilaration is assured. The course is not a parade or a showy processional. It is a course marked by the Cross, but at the finish line we will be embraced by Christ. "Consider Him who endured such opposition from sinful men, so that you will not grow weary and lose heart" (Heb. 12:3).

QUESTIONS FOR DISCUSSION

1. Do you agree that growing older does not guarantee spiritual insight and ethical wisdom?
2. How do you account for Solomon's moral and spiritual decline? Do you face any of the same pressures Solomon faced?
3. How do Christians respond to the moral confusion around them?
4. What lessons should we learn from the wrong-headed activism of Moses, Saul, and Peter?
5. Do you agree that our primary concern should be the ethic behind our ethics?

6. If moral endurance is like a marathon, what are the qualities of character needed in the runner?
7. Do you agree that Jesus is much more than an example to us of how to run the moral marathon?
8. What changes need to take place in your own life to free you from the maze so that you can run with perseverance the race clearly marked out by Christ?

GENERAL INDEX

SCRIPTURE INDEX